W9-BAT-397

THIS IS
NOT
A WINE
GUIDE

CHRIS
MORRISON

———

THIS IS
NOT
A WINE
GUIDE

———

MURDOCH BOOKS

SYDNEY · LONDON

CONTENTS

Foreword

I like a good sommelier. What's not to like about somebody who brings you wine? But even so, when top sommelier Chris Morrison came in to train up a roomful of restaurant reviewers for the Sydney Morning Herald *Good Food Guide* on how to judge a wine list, I just assumed he was going to tell us stuff we already knew. Yawn.

Instead, he woke us up to the fact that wine had changed. He spoke of new varietals (so different from even ten years ago), and new ways of drinking. He talked about the structure of a wine and its relationship with food, and about tricks of the trade that only a somm would know.

Clearly, he has a desperate need to make wine make sense. So we should all be pleased that he has decided to bottle all the stuff he knows into a book that is as refreshing as it is helpful.

Wine writers tend to write from the bottle backwards: the winemaker, the vineyard, the year, the harvest, the philosophy. All good stuff, but sommeliers take it forward as well, dealing more with the experience of drinking it, and why, and with what. Chris is on our side. Wine isn't a product, or a commodity, or something out of reach of mere mortals, but something that simply makes eating more fun. As Chris says, 'wine doesn't make sense without food'.

So this is different from other wine books; a sort of straight-from-the-sommelier's-mouth take on how to create a great experience around wine both in the restaurant and at home. It's about how Australia has changed from a drinking culture to a wine culture; how the old rules of judgement (aroma and flavour) have been replaced by structure and texture; about the merits of wine scoring versus smashability.

Read this book and you will find out how wine gets its colour, why some wines age better than others, why alcohol percentages can't be trusted, and why certain wines make your mouth all furry. But because he's a sommelier, accustomed to talking to chefs about building and layering flavour in a dish, and to diners about skin contact, acidity, tannin; you'll find out so much more. Chris uses food to unlock wine, which to me, as an eater first, drinker second, makes a lot of sense.

I particularly like the quietly subversive ideas planted throughout the book like rosebushes in a vineyard (chilling shiraz knocks back the sweetness; oxidation is all about umami; the 30-second rule when entertaining). I like the section on buying wine, which he divides into Traders, Premiums and Investments, and I like that he updates the tiresome idea of wine-matching to the sort of food we really eat – cured meats, marinated raw fish, charred lamb chops and salty, deep-fried potato chips.

The best thing about Chris Morrison is that he genuinely wants everyone to know as much as he does and to love wine as much as he does. Thanks Chris. We'll do our best.

Terry Durack

Wine – the new rules

I hated my first glass of wine. It was warm and white and sweet and I thought to myself, 'How can anyone drink this stuff?'. I was fifteen and was still convinced that my life involved being a professional footballer, champion golfer or world surfing champion. As someone who has now spent nearly their entire working life in the wine industry, it would appear that life is not without a sense of irony.

As a sommelier, educator, ambassador, writer and judge I have witnessed firsthand the incredible changes in wine over the last two decades. What I have also seen is that even though the way wine is made and consumed has evolved, the language and principles we use to communicate about it have not. I feel it is time for a new approach to wine. One that reflects the contemporary wine marketplace as much as it does the changing tastes of a highly informed and experience-driven wine drinker. Restaurants and wine bars have become the new social rituals for diners and drinkers. The reality that consumers can and will learn more about wine in the context of food and dining has finally arrived.

The inescapable fact about wine is, no matter how hard we try, no matter how evolved our palate becomes, or how broad our knowledge is, wine is an inherently personal experience, which is largely defined by our own sense of taste. This book is about helping you understand and enjoy wine through the prism of your own preferences – how you like to eat, cook and entertain. I want you to feel comfortable that these – and not accumulated, complex threads of knowledge – should always be your starting points. And yes, just like a sommelier, this book is about understanding the finer points of what to serve with what. But we won't be arriving at that point through a technical approach. First and foremost, this is a practical, 'lifestyle' guide to knowing wine. How you actually live should be at the centre of all your wine decisions, because choosing wine, like anything else you choose in your life (a suit, a dress, where to holiday), should be based on your habits and interests, on what you prefer and on your budget. I can't teach you everything there is to know about wine, but what I can do is show you an approach. And I can tell you the questions you should ask along the way, both of yourself and of anybody you buy wine from, so that you can keep learning.

We have a relentless amount of technology available to us today, and it instantly connects everyone to everything at anytime, anywhere. Despite the 'virtualness' of life, we still have a core need to feel tangibly connected to people in a flesh-and-blood sort of a way. We need engagement in actual social rituals to achieve this, and rituals that bring us together physically. Wine and food are so often at the heart of such occasions and it's this aspect that drives me in what I do. I believe wholeheartedly that opening a bottle of wine is not so much about drinking, as it is about sharing a human experience. It's about inviting someone into your home for a meal. It's about signalling trust or celebrating a moment in time. It's about a night out with friends. It's about making memories and marking occasions. With all the shifts, bumps and changes along wine's journey through history, as both a liquid and as an overarching industry, this basic denominator of wine as a conduit for human interaction never changes.

The occasions that bring people together also need the right mix of food and wine. Your birthday, a picnic in the park, a business lunch or a weekend beach barbecue will potentially call for different wines, in the same way that they require different styles of food. As do those formal milestones you celebrate in a fine diner, or at the school reunion lunch in a BYO local bistro. A good knowledge of wine will help you to select the best ones for the occasion and for the menu, as well as the particulars of knowing which ones to serve with what, and when and how to serve them. This has parallels to a sommelier, fiddling with lists and tasting notes in the back-of-house scenario. But your knowledge of wine should remain secondary to the occasion and not intrude upon it. Undoubtedly, that knowledge helps you make solid wine choices, as mine does for me when I'm at work. But it should swiftly take a back seat to the ensuing festivities, dinner or whatever other occasion is at hand.

What I want to convey in this book is that the right approach to wine should create conversation and excitement, not nervousness and fear. In the world of food, entertaining, cooking and dining, wine is not – and never should be – about being bogged down in jargon and pretension and techno speak. I'm hoping this realisation will bring confidence to the wine beginner and give the fully-fledged experts among you something to ponder, too.

THE
SOMMELIER

A good sommelier can take your dining experience to a place so elevated, you feel like you have to peer down over the edge of your table to see heaven. A bad one can make you feel like your wallet has been lifted.

'Sommelier' is a French term referring to a highly trained, extremely knowledgeable wine and drinks professional. While sommeliers are rooted in the history of wine, they work across multiple categories of liquids in restaurants and wine bars – beer, sake, cider, distilled spirits and even non-alcoholic beverages – bringing their expertise to every aspect of service, from conceiving, implementing and maintaining a drinks list, to a thorough knowledge of how to match them with food. For the purposes of this book, the ultimate expression of this is in the food and wine experience on a dining room floor, where a sommelier guides a diner through the process of selecting a wine to accompany their meal. Sommeliers are employed by all kinds of restaurants, but generally those where service and wine budgets are bigger, and the per-head spend is higher. At this kind of restaurant, wine is placed on the same footing as food.

A good sommelier can take your dining experience to a place so elevated, you feel like you have to peer down over the edge of your table to see heaven. A bad one can make you feel like your wallet has been lifted. An impressive wine knowledge is crucial to being a good sommelier – but it's not the whole story. The measure of a great sommelier is as much about the things you can't teach someone, as about the things you can. Humour, a work ethic, decent values and a bit of humility are all vital when you're handling customers. A sommelier needs to be able to connect with people in a genuine manner and find out what they like or want, while making them feel in control of the decision-making. When you're a customer seeking wine advice, you need guidance, not pushing, and to be spoken 'to' and not 'at'.

To many though, the work of the sommelier is veiled in notions of wine wankery and exclusivity. Waistcoated, impenetrable, aloof and not a little terrifying, the vision of the archetypal sommelier, with their 'tastevin' dangling imperiously from their neck and their entire being bristling with vinous superiority, is hardly one of user-friendliness. This is as unfortunate as it is wrong. I believe a sommelier can *make* your dining experience because, ultimately, bringing good wines into play with food, and the way a successful pairing elevates both, is what being a good sommelier is all about.

My view is that a sommelier should treat the restaurant floor more like a living room than a classroom, with all the warmth, friendliness and comfort that this analogy suggests. This approach to both wine and service is always the starting point for my work, and it's the underpinning premise of this book. I think it's instructive to demystify the role of the sommelier here, before we look at anything else to do with wine.

Understanding that being a sommelier is about communication and skills in human connectedness (with a bit of wine nous thrown in!), helps to put wine in its right context. And putting wine in its right context goes most of the way towards understanding it.

Passion for the profession

I literally fell into wine when I took a bartending job at a Sydney restaurant. Until then, I'd had no clue what I wanted to do and the hospitality industry was a good catchment for slightly unfocused people like me.

WINE NOTE

Too many wine professionals regard restaurants as classrooms, treating their clientele like lesser mortals in dire need of a damn good wine education. We've all had that experience, I'm sure, and it's not pleasant.

The money wasn't bad, the work was labour-intensive but fun and it didn't require much thought; unless, as I was to discover, I actually wanted to turn it into a proper career – in which case, it required a great deal of thought and skill. There's a definite craft to being a good hospitality worker, but at that early stage of my career I had little clue of that. In fact, I didn't have much of a clue about a number of things, including wine. That changed fast.

I was on a break one day when I found a wine book in the restaurant office. With time to kill, I thought I'd have a crack at reading it. And I was still reading it 45 minutes later when the sommelier came out to kick my arse for extending smoko beyond the prescribed 10 minutes. On seeing me sitting on an upturned milk crate next to the rancid kitchen bins, hungrily digesting the contents of said wine book, he looked at me with a knowing smile – and that was that. On the very next shift, I was promoted to assistant sommelier.

At the time, the restaurant's sommelier needed a right-hand man and so my new-found passion for wine, and obvious thirst for knowledge, made me the right choice in his eyes. The day after my lucky promotion, I walked into the restaurant feeling about a foot taller. The pride I felt that day, in being able to represent wine on the restaurant floor, is something that has never left me. My training began in earnest and, at first, it was nothing more than 'on the job' learning, where the tempo of service was fast and furious. I had no option but to keep up.

Not really knowing more than what I'd so recently gleaned from that tattered copy of Jancis Robinson's

Wine Course I'd been caught with the previous day,
I quickly became a part of the fledgling Sydney sommelier
community. We were a loosely knit bunch of functioning
alcoholics and wine junkies, still swooning over Marlborough
sauvignon blanc. It was the early '90s and our restaurant
and wine scene was, compared with today, really still in its
infancy in many ways. Many licensed restaurants invested
the bare minimum – both in funds and imagination – in
their wine lists. Despite this, out of that era some of the
great wine programs, wine cultures and wine professionals
were born.

It was a fantastic breeding ground for people hungry to
learn. I remember wine programs such as the one at Cicada
restaurant in Sydney's Potts Point, where I first encountered
a list regarded by those in-the-know as being truly world
class. My first visit to Rockpool, in the heart of Sydney's The
Rocks district, was where I first encountered a well-drilled,
highly trained wine team, bringing a sense of theatre and
flawless choreography to their service. Such experiences
not only inspired me to learn more about wine, but also
fuelled my passion for the profession of serving it.

A valuable education

Two years after the wine book, milk crate and dirty bins
incident, I finished my final shift as assistant sommelier
and was getting ready to leave for London. In the
intervening years my sommelier education had been
somewhat expanded by a guy I consider a mentor.

His name was Kevin, or 'Kev'. He wasn't the sommelier
but a waiter and, as such, considered on the fringes of

WINE NOTE

By the way, I regard tasting wine and general wine education as 'back-of-house' skills, and don't think they should ever encroach on the work done on the restaurant floor. The job on the floor is about giving service first, and being a conduit for food and wine information to the customer. Learning about wine is done behind the scenes and shouldn't infiltrate down to the customer. Knowledge should be worn with confident ease, not used to bang people over the head.

wine service. He didn't really want the responsibility of selling wine to customers, but it was clear that his knowledge of wine, and the wine industry was stronger than anyone else's on the team. He had an incredible palate. His was the type of sensory vocabulary where you could literally throw any wine at him, without showing him the bottle or providing any information about its contents, and he could nail the variety, region and often the exact year of vintage. He took an interest in me, taking time to explain why a particular wine tasted the way that it did, what smells I should look for in a wine and how to discern good ones from bad. Kev taught me about texture and why it is as vital to consider when evaluating a wine, as it is to think about flavour and aroma. He drilled into me the idea that the true potential of wine was only unlocked when consumed with food.

For two years, after every single shift, Kev left a line-up of wines for me to try. They were little tastes, leftovers from bottles sold and served that night – or they were new wines, about to be offered by the glass on the wine list. Sometimes they were from something he had tried that day in a wine sales meeting with the sommelier, who would always call him in to help taste the myriad wine samples. Along with the wines there would be a note from him, urging me to look, smell, taste, think and write something down about each and every wine. These were all served blind. The next day we would discuss my notes and responses while we carried out cellar duties together. He taught me both the importance of a rigorous tasting technique and the appropriate place for wine appreciation and education. To this day I still refer to these lessons. Whenever I'm asked about my 'qualifications' for the senior position I hold now in wine, I can't help but travel back to the moments I spent with this man who, in my eyes, and almost despite himself, had the greatest influence on my career – in ways that perhaps he will never realise, sadly. And, as so often happens in this crazy industry I work in, I lost track of him soon after I went to London.

How things have changed. It seems now whenever I interview a potential applicant for a wine role, they are very eager to skip the movie and head straight to the credits. They can't wait to tell me how they've just attained their Court of Master Sommeliers' qualification, Wine and Spirit Education Trust certificate or even their aspirations to the MW (Master of Wine) – this latter is for the unnaturally gifted only. In reality there are only around 24 MWs in Australia, so the chances of me coming across someone who's just attained theirs, and is applying for a hospo job, is rather low. Anyhow. My point is this: there seems to be an endless selection of tertiary qualifications for those looking to advance or sharpen their wine-career curve. Some hope that a diploma or two will catapult them into a sommelier's position, quick smart. I always hate to tell them that it won't. I'm all for people getting qualifications but, as far as becoming a sommelier is concerned, pieces of paper aren't the whole story.

The hardest part about being a wine professional is that the job, which is largely about honing your own palate and increasing your own wine mastery, is one where you can

I always find that the people I serve in my role respond most positively when I make the conversation relevant to them; it's never about me.

get so wrapped up in the technical aspects that you're in danger of losing respect for someone else's sense of taste. Wearing a badge or gaining a certificate doesn't qualify you to provide good wine service. It's about learning to communicate with someone in order to get across the information required, while making the other party feel part of the process. And that's a fine balancing act. I always find that the people I serve in my role respond most positively when I make the conversation relevant to them; it's never about me.

Having wine knowledge enables me to build a wine list that's clearly linked to the style of a particular venue and its food. It helps me promote an in-house wine culture consistent with the philosophy of that restaurant. But I see too many sommeliers, rabid with opinion and intellect, who simply can't relate to the customer in front of them. In restaurants, when a single bottle of wine can easily cost more than your meal, there is a distinction between service and intrusion, between advising and up-selling. Sommeliers need to remember that it's their floor craft that really sets them apart from the pack, not their prowess in the tasting room. A restaurant wine professional requires a skill-set made up of time-on-the-job plus education, and you can't leapfrog over the former with just a certificate. I get a real thrill seeing a young sommelier embrace opportunities in learning how to handle people, both on the job and from their teammates. I get even more pleasure when they leave and move on to bigger and better things in the industry.

New World upstart

I consider my most valuable 'certificate' to be the one
I earned in London, working for tough French sommeliers.
It wasn't their uncompromising work ethic – or their
seemingly pathological disdain for anyone born outside
France – that made them tough nuts. It was the fierce pride
they took in what they did and their steadfast expectation
that everyone else should have the same level of it.

It was the late 1990s when I arrived in London, full
of stories I'd been fed by colleagues back home, about
the arrogance of French sommeliers. I wanted to work
overseas as I felt it was the best way I could learn
more than was available to me in Australia at the time.
In Australia then, we were making some of our best
wines ... and undeniably some of our worst. In contrast,
London was (and remains) an amazing place for the
wine professional. England has no commercial-scale wine
industry of its own, so it's a beacon for product from
literally all over the wine-producing world. The bar there
is high and the competition tough so the quality of what's
available tends to be impressive. The opportunities to
learn about wine, across the global spectrum and at the
quality end, was immense. So, with a one-way ticket in
one hand and $200 in the other, I arrived in London, filled
with expectations of all that I'd learn.

I took a job at a Conran fine diner called Coq d'Argent.
It was slap bang in London's so-called 'Square Mile' –
the financial heart of the city. The restaurant was one
big transatlantic schmooze fest. London and NYC-based
investment bankers rolled in and out, drunk on the easy

money flowing through the booming financial sector. The role of commis (junior) sommelier was procured for me by chef Michael Moore, then working at Bennelong at the Sydney Opera House, but who'd been Sir Terence Conran's Executive Chef at Bluebird, on Kings Road, Fulham. The Conran group had a love affair with what they called the 'antipodean mafia': 'saffas' from South Africa; 'kiwis' from New Zealand; and Australians, who they called 'skippies'. They loved that we didn't come with Old World hang-ups around working long hours and that, to a person, we were keen to learn.

It was at Coq d'Argent that I first encountered French wine professionals and, as I was to quickly gather, they had their own fixed ideas about New World upstarts. They saw us as representing a wine culture that was loud, brash and somewhat unformed. I came with an accent that butchered the pronunciation of their beloved wines, and that went down ... not so well. They had a 'You know nothing, John Snow' attitude towards me. I was a blow-in from the worst kind of vinous backwater – one they imagined as a sort of geographical mash-up of desert-meets-the-Antarctic.

I decided, despite all their ribbing, to just keep my mouth shut, work hard and absorb absolutely everything I heard, saw and tasted. When there was a conversation about wine, I ensured I was there, soaking everything in. It wasn't until I started working among these London wine teams that I realised being a sommelier was a 'real' job. I remember listening to those experienced guys talk about wine with a passion; it oozed from their conversations.

I also remember the respect they had for each other and how much I wanted that respect too. I knew I had a ton of work to do in order to earn it. I was drawn to the way they had such protective pride in their own wine culture. Little by little, they started to accept me.

After about three months on the job, I arrived at work for lunch service and headed, as I always did, to the cellar to pick up my service toolkit – my sommelier's 'tools of the trade'. Back then, this comprised a 'tastevin' (a small silver cup used to taste wines prior to service, often on a chain hung around the neck), a heavy black apron, two wine knives and a set of wine prongs. There were also three pens and a box of matches to light decanting candles. I walked into the cellar and the entire sommelier team was there, Champagne in hand. The head sommelier, David, looked at me, put his hand on my shoulder and handed me a glass of Champagne. He said, 'Welcome, Chris. *Salut!*' We drank and they all kissed me on both cheeks. Before I could respond, we heard the kitchen team yelling for some coffee, which ended the moment as cleanly as a blow from a sharp chef's knife. The sommelier team filed out of the room one at a time, everyone looking me straight in the eye and shaking my hand. We went directly out onto the floor to deal with a restaurant quickly filling up with diners; the moment was over.

After the drinking–kissing moment, everything changed. It was as though that red velvet VIP rope, designed to keep plebeians out of some exclusive inner sanctum, miraculously opened just for me, and, unbelievably, I was escorted into the 'club'. Suddenly, I didn't head home after work, but was invited out for a drink with the team. I was included in other post-shift rituals too, such as visiting West End wine bars, where we'd throw our night's tips into the middle of a table. We'd add up the cash then someone would order wine and food; each night it was a different person's turn. I still shiver involuntarily when I recall the first time the responsibility of the night's wine fell to me.

Rather than order a wine, I had secretly bought a bottle from a store in Chelsea. It was a 1984 Seppelt sparkling shiraz. Aged sparkling reds are one of Australia's greatest and most unique wines. However, the appearance of shiraz with bubbles is not something the French are accustomed to. At all. The roar of laughter as I poured each of them a frothy glass of fizzy red wine made my stomach drop. But then the food arrived and, after a minute or two of smelling and tasting the wine, the heckling died down and there was silence. One of the sommeliers asked for pinot noir glasses; these have a broad base and a narrow opening and help wine 'open up', becoming more aromatic, complex and flavoursome in the process. After another excruciating minute or two and several plates of food later, the head sommelier looked at me, smiled, and said, 'Well done'. It was the proudest moment of my life.

I was thrilled to work with those French colleagues. I came to deeply respect the way they curate their history and evolution through their gastronomy. This remains a significant inspiration for me. Their culture and passion for food and wine helped shape the approach I use in my profession to this day.

THE SERVICE TOOLKIT

SOMMELIER KNIFE You can spend a fortune on one of these if you choose to, but the best ones are still the simple 'double-pull' wine corkscrews, also known as a waiter's friend or wine key, which you can buy at any kitchen retail outlet. They differ from the standard 'single-pull' corkscrews as they have two hinges, or levers, which enable you to remove the cork with more safety and success. Also, with wines under cork, there will be a plastic or foil sleeve over the top of the bottle. In a restaurant scenario, removing it is the first part of the wine-opening process. A little etiquette is required here. The knife of your corkscrew (good ones are serrated and last longer than non-serrated) goes under the lower of the two lips at the top of the bottle. You run the knife smoothly around the neck in two to three movements. You don't rotate the bottle, as the label always needs to face the guest and you don't want to disturb any sediment. However, for home, my advice for the plastic ones is to grip the entire sleeve in one hand, give it a twist and rip the whole thing off! No need to stand on ceremony. For a foil sleeve, take the knife from your corkscrew and make a cut down the side of the sleeve, from top to base, and peel it away slowly.

The 1-2-3 of the double-pull wine corkscrew:

1. Screw the corkscrew into the cork, then position the first lever on the lip of the bottle.
2. Pull the corkscrew up until the second lever is in line with the lip of the bottle.
3. Position the second lever on the lip of the bottle and pull the cork up and out of the bottle.

WINE PRONGS This device has a handle and two thin, flat metal bands and it sort of looks like a tuning fork. The metal bands are gently forced down the neck of the wine bottle, down either side of the cork, then carefully twisted and pulled to encourage the cork out of the bottle. This is a great tool for older wines whose corks may have become brittle over time.

GOOD DECANTERS The humble decanter is the sommelier's best friend, for pouring wine into for aeration and also for seasoning glasses. (See pages 189–92 for more information on seasoning and decanters.)

A TASTING GLASS I keep one of these with me at all times when opening and serving wines. I use it to taste wines prior to serving to ensure they're in good condition. Avoid using a small, short glass with a narrow body and base. This type of glass won't allow the wine to 'open up' and express itself. I use a glass that is broad in the base so the wine is exposed to more oxygen. This will also quickly expose any faults in the wine. Aromas and flavours will also emerge faster, so I can make a quick assessment of the total quality of the wine before I serve the customer.

POLISHING CLOTH Always have one of these on hand, especially if you plan on changing glassware during the meal. Cloths should be clean, dry and lint-free.

LIGHT I have always worked with some source of direct light, such as a slow-burning decanting candle and matches, a small flashlight or even a cigarette lighter. Why?

• Using direct light to backlight a wine while in the bottle can allow you to detect levels of sediment.

- When decanting, backlighting the shoulder and neck of the wine bottle shows you when sediment is at risk of escaping the bottle into your decanter. (See page 202 for more information on removing sediment from a wine.)

NOTEBOOK I still carry one of these if I work on the restaurant floor, and use it to record the details of wines I have tasted and food they worked well with. When serving wine at home, you can also make notes that strike a chord with you, maybe either because you liked the wine or you didn't. You don't need to draft an essay, just take a note of:

- Tasting date (important if you are cellaring the wine)
- Name of wine, grape variety, region and/or vineyard
- What you liked about the wine
- What you didn't like about the wine
- What you drank it with (food-wise) and how it worked
- Importantly, write these notes in YOUR words – don't reach for language, terms and descriptors that you see in professional reviews. This will help to improve your wine vocabulary, as well as your palate. Focus on the basic tastes, body, texture and mouthfeel, which we discuss in The fundamentals of wine chapter.

SOMEWHERE TO PUT RUBBISH Opening wine can be a messy business, so having a small container to put the screw-caps, corks, or any other debris associated with wines being opened and tasted is highly recommended.

It's not about you

Money was easy back then, and so were the wine sales.
I remember a group of young bucks coming in for a Friday
lunch. They sat down, loud and full of confident swagger.
The host of the table asked for the wine list immediately
and I could tell they were on the hunt for something big. In
my mind I gave the host the title 'Big Dog'. I smelled more
than a touch of arrogance. Bonus season was here and
they wanted to celebrate. I heard the unmistakable snap
of fingers – that snap that's meant to say to service staff,
'Get here now!'– and whenever I hear it, it never fails to
curdle my blood. Summoning all my dignity, I approached
the table and put on my most professional 'Yes sir, how
can I help you?' air. Big Dog didn't even look up from the
wine list to meet my gaze. 'What's your best wine?' he
demanded. I pointed out several options at various price
points, taking in a bit of grape variety and regional variation
along the way, with nothing priced over £150. He stopped
me mid-sentence. 'Mate,' he said, looking at me this time
with disdain. 'I asked what is your BEST wine?' 'You might
like this sir,' I answered – code for 'OK arsehole, cop this'.
Flicking wine list pages furiously, I pointed at our red
Bordeaux selection. 'The 1945 Château Mouton Rothschild,'
I purred, thinking, at £2850, that I'd really put him in his
place. 'Done!' he said, exultantly, while I looked down to
catch the exact moment the wine list was snapped shut
and thrust into my stomach.

Big Dog re-engaged in conversation with the rest of the
table, roaring with laughter and high-fiving all his guests.
I rushed to the cellar and gently drew the wine from a

particularly dark corner, reserved for the oldest and rarest.
I returned to the table and presented the wine carefully,
reading its label aloud, confirming the selection was correct.
With reverence, I carried the bottle to the sommeliers'
station, a long wooden bench that held our toolkits and
decanters. I then began the delicate process of decanting
the wine. When dealing with such an aged wine, it's a crucial
moment in service. It's not just about separating wine from
the sediment, but also about measuring how the wine is
reacting to its sudden exposure to oxygen after so many
years. If the wine is past its best, and this happens, it will
literally 'fall apart' at this point, losing its aroma, flavour and
complexity. If the wine is still in good nick, though, it will
actually gain these characteristics, increasing in them the
longer it is in the decanter. To my relief, the wine was sound
and was starting to 'open up' nicely. I took the decanter
to the table and poured five perfect glasses. I stood back
and watched them smell the wine, eyes closed, lost in
those heady and inviting aromas. Without warning, they
all stood up and touched raised glasses. Then, as a group,
they downed the entire contents in a single gulp. I made a
noise that sounded like a cross between a cat hissing and
the squealing sound that air makes when you slowly let it
out of a balloon. Recovering from the shock of such flagrant
guzzling of a wine that deserved reverence and awe, I again
heard the snap of fingers and felt Big Dog eyeing me from
across the room. 'Again!' he said.

Not all days were heady like this but, suffice to say, the
wines we served routinely were extremely high quality and
largely European. The people who drank them were wealthy

and not concerned about price, but were conscious of status. London had a lot to offer but it was also a finishing school for a Masters in Wine Pretentiousness. By the time London had finished with me, I'd graduated from being an antipodean 'yob' to a full-blown 'snob'.

Ultimately, I settled back into Sydney, taking a job at Bel Mondo restaurant. It was an Italian fine diner run by legendary chef Stefano Manfredi. His mother, Franca, would make fresh pasta every day on a flour-coated trestle table, right in front of the kitchen. The food was exciting, but I had come back home to Australia full of self-importance.

One Friday night, the usual crowd was arriving for dinner, a mix of locals, tourists and city professionals and, at one of my tables, sat two women and three men. After considering the wine list for five minutes, the host of this suited assortment called me over and ordered a heavily wooded chardonnay, pointing determinedly to a commercial wine that hovered around the $90 mark. Right about now my work in London resurfaced in a spectacular combination of indignation and arrogance. Navigating to another section of the list with such speed and force that I nearly sent the guy's designer glasses flying, my finger fell on my selection. I looked at the host, visibly screwed up my face and said, 'Sir, this wine is, I think, closer to what you are after. It has the characteristics of oak and malolactic fermentation you are asking for, but is a far better choice.' I went on, intoning at length about lactic acid and butter, softness, richness and roundness. I still remember the tense pause that drew out after I'd spoken. It was as excruciating as that silence that descends in a Western movie, after 'the kid' enters the

saloon and the piano player stops dead. My guy pointed
again to his original choice on the wine list and insisted,
'that one'. After something of a Mexican standoff, in the
end he went with my suggestion. I left the table feeling
satisfied I'd given my guest a much-needed lesson in
wine appreciation.

I didn't think much more about the incident until I was
called into the restaurant office the next morning to report
to the head sommelier. He was small and French and
frustrating, but he was a small and French and frustrating
sommelier in Australia – which, at that time, made him a
god. 'We received a complaint about you from a guest
last night,' he said without looking up from his computer.
Followed by, 'You're fired'. The chardonnay guy, I figured.
I didn't know what to say and I didn't really know what I
had done wrong. As I was leaving, he gave me a one-line
piece of advice that would come to define my entire work
philosophy from that point. I still stick by it today. *Mon ami,*
he said. 'Remember this. As a sommelier it is never, ever,
about you. It's about your customer.'

I'd become that very thing I most loathed, and everything
that this book is not about. Namely, a wine wanker. Getting
the boot and learning that hard lesson set me on a course
from which I've never deviated in all my decades of
professional wine work.

On restaurant floors, I see plenty of sommeliers who
remind me of myself back then. Oblivious to the customer.
Intent on impressing with what they know. Selling wine
to unsuspecting diners based on a certain personal belief
system rather than taste. But, as we've seen, being a

An open mind is one of the greatest assets you can cultivate on your journey of learning about wine.

sommelier is a customer-based service profession, not a blind-you-with-science kind of one. The challenge always remains that, when I walk onto the restaurant floor, it is no longer about me, but about the person at the other end of the wine bottle.

How does all of this relate to you at home? Actually, in much the same way as it does in a restaurant. Accumulating wine knowledge is a good thing, as I mentioned, but it shouldn't get in the way of the occasion – or the food – that you bring the wine out for. You should feel confident in your own knowledge and wine decisions and understand, too, that learning about wine is a never-ending, life-long process. Along the way you'll learn from others who will have their own unique spin on the subject. An open mind is one of the greatest assets you can cultivate on your journey of learning about wine; that and an appreciation for the fact that you'll never completely 'arrive'. There's so much to know and you'll never fully know it all.

THE FUNDAMENTALS
OF WINE

Before we go any further, it might be useful to discuss a few fundamentals about wine and clarify some important terminology that I use throughout this book. I will only list what I think is vital to know, and leave out everything that isn't, so you don't get bogged down. Essentially, by sharing with you the most useful things that I've learned from my experience as a wine professional and sommelier, I want to help you build a tasting toolkit, including how to describe basic wine styles; a simple understanding of texture; what 'body' in wine means and why it's important; the building blocks of wine; blended wine; and why some wines age and others don't. I'll also touch on some of the basic winemaking principles that are improving the wines you drink today in restaurants, so you know how to ask for them. The following pages are here to guide, encourage and answer your questions – just as I would if I was having a glass of wine with you, or taking care of you in a restaurant as your sommelier.

Basic types of wine

There are six basic types of wine:

SPARKLING WINE All wines with bubbles, including Champagne and prosecco.

WHITE WINE Wines that have pale green, yellow and gold colours. White wines can be made from the juice of black or white grapes.

RED WINE Wines that are made from dark-skinned grape varieties.

ROSÉ Wines that are made by either blending white and red wines, or by soaking grape juice from dark-skinned grapes and their skins together for a very short amount of time. They are normally pink.

DESSERT WINE All wines that have residual sugar (RS). RS refers to any sugar left in a wine after alcoholic fermentation is complete. (See page 45 for more information on alcoholic fermentation.)

FORTIFIED WINE Port, sherry, Madeira, vermouth and marsala are all examples of fortified wine. Alcohol is added to these wines in the middle of the fermentation process. This stops the yeast from converting sugar to alcohol and not only leaves residual sugar (RS) in the wine, but increases the wine's final alcohol levels.

Body

In simple language, when talking about wine, the term 'body' is related to the concentration of sugar, acid and tannin in the grapes. How this impacts your wine selection and the food, occasion and people you will match it with, starts with you. There are no 'rights' or 'wrongs' with body in a wine, except when it relates to food – it's how you utilise a wine's body with food that ultimately triggers it into play. Without food in the mix, discussions about body are just academic.

The three categories of body are light, medium and full. I'm reluctant to give examples here under each type of body, as I don't want to cloud the issue. The grape varieties that are available have changed enormously over the last two decades and the range is now so complex. To single a few out in this discussion is a bit token, but I've given you a few anyway by way of illustration, rather than making any gospel-like statements. Your perception of texture can be personal, but this topic is way less subjective than is the can of worms that is flavour and aroma combinations, which I discuss in the Old rules, new thinking chapter.

... 'body' is related to the concentration of sugar, acid and tannin in the grapes.

LIGHT-BODIED

Light-bodied wines will have very light colouring. They are delicate and clean-tasting and exhibit lower concentrations of alcohol and tannin. Generally, they will be un-oaked and will have pronounced or, at least, high acidity. The resulting wines will be quite dry. Whites in this category can include riesling, pinot grigio and vermentino, while reds can include gamay and pinot noir.

MEDIUM-BODIED

Medium-bodied wines will have a more intense, deeper colouring, and will also have more weight and texture and a higher concentration of alcohol, as well as firmer, often savoury, tannins, and generally some influence from oak. Some possible white examples are pinot gris, semillon

HOW DOES WINE GET ITS COLOUR?

If you took a red grape like shiraz and a white grape like riesling and squeezed them, the juice that would come out is almost the same colour – a greenish-grey liquid. Wine gets most of its colour from contact with the grape skins. White wine grapes are separated from their skins early in the winemaking process to keep the colour clean and bright (except for skin-contact whites, see page 139). Red wines result from the juice and skins of the grape 'soaking' together. This is where a shiraz gets its deep, dark colour.

and sauvignon blanc. Grenache is a good example of a medium-bodied red.

FULL-BODIED

Full-bodied wines come with deep, dense colouring and are generally made from grapes grown in warm to hot regions. Therefore, they will have high concentrations of alcohol, increased weight, texture and mouthfeel, higher levels of fruit character and a softer acidity. New oak will generally play a more pivotal role in full-bodied wines, as the powerful aromas and flavours of new oak find balance with the higher concentration of this type of wine. Full-bodied red wines will have increased tannins. An example of a full-bodied white wine is chardonnay, while shiraz is a classic example of a full-bodied red.

Balance

When you taste a wine, what sticks out about it? If the answer is 'nothing' and you are enjoying the wine, then there is a good chance that what you are experiencing is a well-balanced wine. If individual elements, such as the tannins, the acidity, alcohol or the sweetness, are dominant and you are not enjoying the wine, there is every possibility that it's out of balance. (See pages 48, 74 and 225 for more information on balance.)

Texture and mouthfeel

This is the sum of the physical or tactile components of a wine, or what you would also call 'mouthfeel'. Parts of a wine that contribute to texture are tannin, alcohol, sugar (sweetness) and acidity. For example, a high-acid wine would be 'crisp'; a low-tannin, fruity red like pinot noir could be called 'supple'; or a high-tannin, high-alcohol red could be called 'rich'. Importantly, the words that you will use to describe texture in wine are already in your vocabulary – you probably use them to describe food. The words we use to describe texture are more uniform than those used to describe flavour and aroma, and therefore are easier to share and understand with others.

> Importantly, the words that you will use to describe texture in wine are already in your vocabulary — you probably use them to describe food.

Sweetness

What is sweet wine and what is dry wine? 'Dry' is a term for a wine where all the sugar has been converted into alcohol during fermentation. Therefore the wine will have no apparent 'sweetness' on the palate. The term 'dry' can apply to sparkling, white, pink and red wines. It usually won't apply to sweet or fortified wines as those require residual sugar to be included in the final style of wine. Sweet wines are those that taste sweet, and sweetness can be found in any wine if the winemaker chooses to include it in the final wine style. However, it only suits specific wines, including grape varieties like riesling and the aforementioned wine styles like sweet or fortified wines. It's important to remember that 'sweet' is different from 'fruity'.

Fruit concentration

I believe that if a wine is made from a certain fruit, that fruit should be evident in the final wine. However, what is important is that the concentration, or intensity, of that fruit character is in harmony with the other elements of the wine – primarily acidity, tannin and alcohol. For me, fruit concentration is the measure of a wine's intensity of flavour, not the type of flavour. A fruity wine like sauvignon blanc from New Zealand, for instance, must have equally concentrated acidity to balance it. A powerfully built shiraz from the Barossa Valley should be supported by strong tannins to create a platform for the intense dark fruit flavours associated with these wines. The better integrated the acidity and tannin are into the wine's fruit concentration, the better the final wine will taste.

Tannin

Tannin is a compound found in the skin, stalk and seeds of grapes, as well as in oak. Tannins in wine give us that dry, 'furry', feeling in the mouth. Many of us have been programmed to respond to cheap, soft, 'slurpable' wines with a pleasant kick of alcohol and sweetness – these aren't necessarily bad things, mind you. But it's the tannin in a wine that makes food come alive. Tannin makes fats recede and promotes that savoury aspect of a wine, where flavours are pushed across and over the back of your palate, creating 'length' (see page 75) and leaving your mouth refreshed. Tannins can also be present in oak.

There are almost as many levels of tannins as there are flavours and aromas in wine. The winemaker will judge how much tannin goes into the finished wine, monitoring the amount of time that skins, seeds and juice remain in contact. Red wines have high concentrations of tannin, whose function goes beyond adding flavour and structure to a wine; it also acts like a natural preservative. (Note that

Tannin is a compound found in the skin, stalk and seeds of grapes, as well as in oak. Tannins in wine give us that dry, 'furry', feeling in the mouth.

acidity is another natural preservative in wine.) Tannins are also an antioxidant and their job is largely to control the process of oxidation in the wine. If oxygen gets into the wine too quickly (without enough tannin and acid to protect it), then the wine will oxidise to the point where the flavours become spoiled. As you can see, tannins are rather crucial in winemaking.

Acidity

Acidity in wine relates to the crispness, tartness and, sometimes, sour characteristics. It's what gives wine its 'backbone', its structure and freshness. Acidity in red wine has always played second fiddle to tannin. Tannins add texture and weight, while acidity cuts and refreshes. Tannin in the right measure can help fill out a wine, making it more powerful and robust, while acidity can elongate the palate, creating elegance. Tannins in the wrong proportions, be they too little or too much, can also dilute or overwhelm the natural flavour of the grape variety and the resulting wine. Acidity in the wrong proportion can leave a wine flabby and lifeless, or hard and tart. (It would be fair to say that I have a real addiction to acidity in wine – probably as a coping mechanism for my addiction to salty, fatty foods!)

Oak

The practice of storing wine in oak goes back thousands of years. Initially this was done for practical reasons, such as transportation and storage. But over the centuries, winemakers and drinkers slowly caught on to the fact that oak imparted aroma, flavour, weight and mouthfeel to a wine. The rest, as they say, is history and oak is now an important component in winemaking. The basic rule regarding concentration of oak character in wine is the younger and smaller the 'format' of the oak (meaning, the size of the oak barrel), the more oak you will notice in the wine. This is a volume thing – the smaller the vessel, the more wine will be in direct contact with it. Oak vats in many northern Italian wineries, for example, can hold 10,000 litres (2600 gallons). Barrels used by the Champagne house Krug hold just 205 litres (54 gallons). The potential of oak is realised when it achieves balance with the natural characters in a wine, such as taste, flavour and aroma.

WINE AND BODY IMAGE

When thinking about dry wine, it's interesting to use the following analogy. Consider tannin, acidity, sweetness and alcohol as parts of the human body. Acidity is like the skeleton and nervous system – it gives a wine structure and definition. Tannins are the muscle and tendons, to build strength and potency. Sweetness is flesh – it lays a softness and tenderness over the structural components of a wine. Alcohol in wine is like sugar in food. It hits your body's 'problem area' – alcohol is wine's version of a 'love handle' or 'muffin top'. Excessive alcohol adds a soft, gooey texture to wine, as it is usually derived from grapes that are very ripe. A 'healthy body' in wine needs the same features as a healthy human body.

While it is still used widely, there's a move away from the obtrusiveness of new oak. More winemakers are pulling back on the percentage of oak in their wines, in order to showcase more of the grape and the vineyard character. Oak will generally only be used in wines that can absorb it, and these tend to be higher in alcohol and richer in fruit character. They can handle the powerful oak flavours and the increase in body and texture that oak lends. When drinking a wine, always remember that if you can taste the oak, there's been too much of it used. Light-bodied wines will generally be un-oaked because oak aromas and flavours can overwhelm their delicate nature. Oaked wines tend to come from warmer climates, where medium- to full-bodied wines deliver mouth-filling and intense flavours.

ALCOHOL IS JUST A NUMBER

The alcoholic percentage you see on a wine label isn't quite accurate. Many countries, including the big wine nations like France, Italy and Spain, along with New World countries like Australia and the USA, can have misleading percentages on labels. There can be a 0.5 to 1.5 per cent variation in the actual alcohol level, compared with the number on the label. The 13.5 per cent chardonnay you are buying could have up to a 15 per cent alcohol content. Don't buy wine based on alcohol percentages. If you pick up alcohol in a dry or sweet wine (see Alcohol, opposite) it is a fault. However, you should be able to detect it in fortified wine, as added alcohol is an integral part of the finished wine in that case.

Alcohol

Alcoholic fermentation is the process whereby sugar is converted into alcohol with the aid of yeast. It makes sense that the more sugar a grape contains, the more alcohol will be produced in the resulting wine through fermentation. Warm climates naturally produce grapes with more sugar, therefore warm-climate wines are generally higher in alcohol. This leads to increased weight and texture in the wines, too. Cooler climates provide less potential for sugar in grapes, translating to less potential alcohol. For this reason, cool-climate wines are usually lower in alcohol, and subsequently can be lighter in body. Remember that alcohol is just a number on the back of the bottle – it will give you no real idea of what a wine will taste like. It's not an indicator of quality either – although wines with alcohol that's out of balance can taste 'hot' and acidic. I've had 17 per cent alcohol wine-beasts that tasted fresh, and 13 per cent alcohol wines that smelled like vodka when I opened them. As well as 'hot', certain alcohols can come across as soft and smooth, and winemakers can exploit this to enhance desirable characteristics in a wine. When alcohol is in balance in a wine, it should produce a pleasant 'warmth'.

Lees

Lees are dead yeast cells and they play a natural part in the winemaking process. When yeast finishes its job of converting sugar into alcohol during fermentation, the dead yeast cells fall to the bottom of the vessel in which the fermentation took place. This could be an oak barrel, a stainless steel tank or even the wine bottle itself. As they accumulate, the dead cells form a milky substance called 'lees', and they've become a handy tool for winemakers looking to add texture, mouthfeel and complexity to a wine, without having to risk overdosing the wine on oak. The amount of lees character a wine will exhibit largely depends on the amount of time the wine spends in contact with the yeast lees prior to final bottling. As well as imparting flavour qualities, lees are also an antioxidant and help preserve freshness during the maturation phase. You'll detect lees in a wine when you perceive a creamy texture across the mid palate; lees-affected wines should always retain some refreshing acidity.

One of the most famous examples of a lees-affected wine is Muscadet sur lie from Muscadet in Brittany, on France's northwest coast. It matures on lees prior to bottling and the result is a particularly light-bodied, fresh, tangy wine with a gorgeously creamy texture. It's known as 'fisherman's wine' because it's such a perfect accompaniment to the crustaceans, shellfish, oysters and fish the region produces.

It's interesting to note that historically, adding anything to white wine, including lees, was regarded as adding 'imperfections'. The object was always to separate the juice from the skins and solids as quickly as possible and make wines that were utterly pristine – no lees, no oxidising, no tannins. In the last 20 to 30 years we've seen a major shift away from this purist approach, with lees, skin contact and tannins being encouraged in white winemaking. The results are, in my opinion, wines that are way more interesting with food.

Age

Most wines are not destined to have a particularly long life; the majority are consumed on the same day they're purchased. So they're not exactly hanging around in cellars collecting bottle age. But the high concentrations of acidity and tannin that enhance a wine's 'drinkability' (see also page 68) when it's young, also give it the stamina to age. Over time, the large moving pieces of fruit and alcohol are supported by acidity and tannin and, when in the right proportions, a wine will evolve into a multi-faceted, finely layered masterpiece of texture, taste and aroma. Wines with age will have greater complexity, as time breaks down the tannins, softening them. They become softer and more savoury versions of their younger selves. It's hard to find a good and affordable collection of aged wines in restaurants and wine bars. No sommelier or restaurateur in their right mind buys a wine and then says, 'I need to wait five years before I can sell this!' The real value behind ageing wine is when you do it yourself (see page 222).

AGEING WINE

We do discuss this in great depth in the Collecting wine chapter, but here I'll say this much: the key to successfully ageing wine lies in finding that balance between sugar, acid and tannin. A good example of a wine that ages well is a full-bodied shiraz from the warm climate of South Australia's Barossa Valley, renowned for its ability to age. At their best, these wines have high and balanced concentrations of fruit, oak, alcohol, acidity and texture. The key to a great ageing wine is having all these

No sommelier or restaurateur in their right mind buys a wine and then says, 'I need to wait five years before I can sell this!' The real value behind ageing wine is when you do it yourself.

characteristics present in similar quantities; the alcohol should be high, but so should the concentration of oak. Fruit character, and the natural acidity required to balance it, is also vital. The same theory holds for a wine at the complete opposite end of the spectrum – for example, the light-bodied, 'wiry' and crisp rieslings from the Eden Valley, also in South Australia. Low in alcohol but intensely flavoured, these rieslings have little-to-no tannin but are remarkably high in natural acidity. They zip down your palate like a laser. Eden Valley's cool climate is perfect for producing wine that's light-bodied, well-proportioned and with the delicate and refreshing mouthfeel and texture suitable for the long haul in your cellar.

THE IMPORTANCE OF BALANCE IN AGEING WINE

A wine needs balance between all the elements of taste; elements that can not only make the wine drink well young, but give it the potential to age. If you have a wine that has a lot of oak, that oak can only work if there is enough fruit to support it. If you have a wine singing with high acidity, it too can work but only if there is fruit flavour to support that acid. On the reverse side, a wine can have lots of fruit flavour but if it doesn't have the support of tannin and/ or acidity, it will be simple and sweet and not suitable for long-term drinking. It's always about balance. Balance is something more than taste, too. When a wine ages, there is a textural, tactile effect that you can detect long before you begin the subjective exercise of evaluating its flavour and aroma.

Freshness

What is 'freshness' in a wine? I get asked this all the time. And although it's an abstract idea, it's important as it keeps coming up in reviews, on wine list descriptions, in marketing speak and so on. A wine is considered 'refreshing' when it feels cleansing in your mouth and is more-ish. A fresh wine won't be sweet or oaky and will be really compatible with food. A refreshing wine won't be too dry or too fruity either; it can be full flavoured but will still have refreshing qualities. The flavours of the grape are in just the right places. If you're still not sure what freshness in a wine is, then know this: a wine with the right amount of it will be one that screams out for food. Freshness doesn't come down to a region or climate, it's more about the invigorating effects a wine has on your palate and the way it behaves with food.

Ripeness

For a grape grower and winemaker, measuring ripeness in wine is like using a builder's spirit level. Imagine that ideal ripeness is when the bubble lines up perfectly between the black lines, with 'underripe' and 'overripe' lying outside the lines. In each vintage there is a constant tweaking and nudging of vines by the growers, to ensure that grapes meet the winemaker's ripeness specifications. The best way I know to describe what a good level of ripeness tastes like in wine, is to imagine biting into a perfectly ripe piece of fruit. It's sweet and fresh at the same time, not sour and not cloying. After you swallow, the memory of that fruit's flavour remains in your mouth but your palate feels clean – not fogged with sugar and not puckering with the dreaded acids of underripeness. It's exactly the same with a wine made from grapes at their peak of ripeness.

If a wine is made using overripe grapes, it's like eating strawberry jam when all you really want is a perfectly ripe strawberry. The first is loaded with sugar and has a cloying texture, with little or no acidity. The latter has lively, aromatic, crisp, red fruit flavours and a lingering acidity that cleans and refreshes your palate. Now imagine this same scenario in terms of conveying the flavours of a grape and its region. It's those fresh, fruity notes, not the jammy ones, that carry the message best. Overripe wines can actually taste appealing (in the same way that confectionery does), but they are suited to immediate drinking and not to ageing.

Underripe wines are at the other end of the flavour spectrum. As I love food analogies when discussing wine, this time we're going to buy two green bananas in order to understand this point. When you get your underripe bananas home, bite into one immediately and make a mental note of its taste and texture. Two to three days later, as the skin takes on a deeper yellow and the fruit softens, bite into that remaining banana and again make mental notes of its texture and flavours. What you are tasting is the difference between underripe or 'green' texture and flavour, and 'ripe' texture and flavour. Wines that have a green character are not the ones that will generally age well, while the ripe ones will go on to live long and happily in your wine collection. I'm telling you this with a caveat, though – I don't want you to get too caught up in ripeness. If you focus on it too much, you risk becoming one dimensional in your vocabulary and emphasis.

Blended wines

Blending is used to augment the character of a wine.
When done right, it will enhance a wine's colour, reshape
its texture and mouthfeel and can even make changes to
aroma and flavour. For example, if a wine lacks a certain
aroma or flavour, a winemaker can 'blend in' a small
percentage of another grape variety with a high level of
that aroma or flavour. Or perhaps that same wine might
lack the right levels of tannin. A winemaker can then add
a percentage of wine from a grape with high concentrations
of tannin. Wines used in blending not only include different
grape varieties, but also wines made from the same grapes,
but ones that have been picked at different stages of
ripeness – be they from different vineyards or aged in oak
or stainless steel tanks. They all bring something to the
blended party.

Centuries ago in European vineyards, it was
commonplace to have several different grape varieties
planted within the boundaries of a single vineyard.
Traditionally, many blended wines emerged from regions
where the climate or prevailing weather meant that a
single grape was unappealing on its own. Blending was the
solution for making a wine more palatable and complete
– like the pieces of a jigsaw coming together. For instance,
cabernet sauvignon on its own can be very 'chewy' with
tannin, especially when made in cooler climates. But if you
blend in a little merlot, the whole wine changes. Merlot
has low tannins, a soft, cuddly texture and juicy flavours,
which fill out and soften the unyielding, tannic nature of
the cabernet sauvignon.

GSM – THE BUSINESS

Easy drinking and particularly juicy, the red blends made from grenache, shiraz and mourvèdre are what we call 'GSMs'. Originally from the warm, sultry climate of the southern Rhône Valley in France, these wines are supple, fresh, full-flavoured and soft in tannin. They can take on nearly any style of food, suit any occasion and are generally very fairly priced. This is because the blending process often uses less than perfect grapes, so production costs are lower and this is reflected in the final price to you or me.

The intention behind many blends today is to do with releasing wine for early, easy drinking. Blending gives winemakers flexibility and the opportunity to 'style' their wines. More winemakers are styling wines today around what they like to eat and the trends are towards 'smashable' or easy-to-drink wines. The contemporary idea of blending wines is becoming more innovative in its approach.

FIELD BLENDS

These are wines made from a single vineyard, where all the vines lying within the boundaries are harvested and blended together, regardless of variety. This is a very traditional way of growing grapes for winemaking. Before wines were styled for mass consumption as they are today, many vineyards were actually composites of multiple grape varieties, planted over decades and, in some cases, centuries. They all got chucked into the winemaking vats together. Modern, mass winemaking doesn't like this approach as it results in wines that are unpredictable in specific flavour and aroma. There's a loss of control at play. However, in the spirit of everything old being new again, more winemakers and grape growers are reviving the idea of field blends as they represent the true heart of a vineyard, built up over time. All those interplanted vines contribute somehow to the final blend. Grapes can be red and white, and the wines either light-, medium- or full-bodied. Importantly, ask for these wines by 'style' and 'body' not by variety or region. An example would be to say, 'I would like a white field blend that is light and fresh'.

Using your knowledge in the real world

This chapter is about distilling the complex language of wine into a collection of terms that can start conversations, and that you can use in real life to help you understand and articulate your own sense of taste. The real test will be when you go out and buy wine – it could be in your local fine wine retailer, a supermarket, online, in a wine bar or restaurant. What I hope is that when you see a sommelier approaching you, or are staring at a wine list, a shelf in a wine shop or at a computer screen, you are filled with confidence and excitement, rather than trepidation and anxiety.

OLD RULES,
NEW THINKING

... honing in on texture and mouthfeel makes wine way more approachable for the punter, whereas the myriad possibilities around flavour descriptors can leave drinkers feeling lost.

I was having lunch with two winemaking friends recently. They were saying how their winemaking was evolving more around how they personally like to eat, and food compatibility was becoming such an important element in their work. They expressed a frustration about the language that currently hovers around wine, explaining how there is too much focus on specific flavours and aromas, and how this tends to confuse people. In their minds there's a need to make, and talk about, wines based around concepts such as texture and mouthfeel, rather than individual flavours and aromas. They argued that honing in on texture and mouthfeel makes wine way more approachable for the punter, whereas the myriad possibilities around flavour descriptors can leave drinkers feeling lost. I thought about our discussion and was heartened by the way their thinking aligned exactly with my own.

Winemakers are important because, like chefs with food, they're at the frontline of wine evolution. If they're shifting in the way they approach wine, it makes sense we can expect exciting changes in winemaking as a result. And, in the same way a chef is driven by their own palate and personal food philosophy when they create a dish or a menu, it makes sense that winemakers ultimately make wines THEY like to consume – wines that reflect their dining style and dining philosophy. My lunch conversation cemented my belief that the approach of chefs, winemakers and sommeliers is coming ever closer together, and that we are all part of the exact same food–wine dialogue.

Of course, aroma and flavour are important, there is no escaping that fact. However, instead of getting caught up in the minutiae of the endless possibilities across the spectrum of flavour, it's better to go the route of the five basic tastes of sour, sweet, salty, bitter and umami, as well as texture and mouthfeel. The five basic tastes are the building blocks of making wine and are, of course, fundamental to food, too. We'll go into them in more detail in the next chapter, but file this away for now. The five basic tastes are the common link between wine and food and the easiest way to create a connection between them. In a way, this link is made tangible in the way the sommelier forms a bridge between a chef and the winemaker. Both the winemaker in their vineyard and the chef in their kitchen have exactly the same mindset about building a wine or a dish. The same language should filter through both scenarios, reflecting the way that both wine and food are similarly tactile and are parts of our general lifestyle.

Getting back to the basics of taste and texture, by focusing on simple elements like acidity, tannin, fruit concentration, balance, body and mouthfeel, actually simplifies wine. These elements are like the vowels of the alphabet. They're easy to remember, and everything else you need to know about a wine stems from understanding them.

Rebooting the way we talk about wine

I think words used to describe food and wine should be the same, not divergent. Think about that for a moment – it's a bit of a revelation. There are a few reasons why we think wine commands a separate, and often impenetrable, vocabulary. In part, it's because wine writers and experts (including many sommeliers) have, historically, used complex and subjective, flowery language to pontificate over wine. We look to these experts to inform us and, if they are talking in this way, it stands to reason that so should we. But you can build your own wine skills and perceptions around your own tastes. You can confidently add to your own understanding. Sure, it's helpful to follow certain wine writers and influencers; but look for ones whose outlook and conclusions align with your taste (I talked more about this in The fundamentals of wine). What I'm aiming to give you instead is a useful 'tasting toolkit' – a way to consider wine in simple terms, and one that will help you unlock it in a user-friendly and food-friendly way.

Much of the language traditionally used around wine has never been updated and this serves to instill doubt in us at a very core level. There have never been more great-quality wines available at excellent prices at any other time in wine's long history. There is literally a wine for everyone and for every occasion. Yet we still trip up when trying to communicate our personal wine tastes, often getting tongue-tied and drawing blanks. This is precisely where the conversation needs to be updated.

In previous eras, wine communication was mainly concerned with the following:

FLAVOUR AND AROMA

As the lunching winemakers highlighted, the communication around wine has always been heavily focused on descriptions of flavour and aroma. And in this, we're not talking about a few flavours and aromas but a

ASK QUESTIONS

Any time I attend a wine lecture or formal tasting, I'm reminded of how far we still need to go. Invariably, speakers will wind up by asking attendees if they have any questions or observations, and just as invariably, everyone in the room seems to freeze in collective fear. No one wants to be 'wrong', so few people ever venture an opinion. I always want to applaud anyone who bravely raises their hand to ask or share something.

complexity of thousands. Listen to any expert talk about a wine and, before long, you're in the realms of 'truffles', 'wet concrete after rain', 'coffee, cherries and sun-ripened fruits' and whatever other flowery descriptors they chuck its way. In my mind, this language constitutes distracting white noise around wine and I find myself pondering that it's no wonder people get confused, and even intimidated, by the subject.

I'll bet many of you know whether you like a wine within seconds of drinking it. But I'll also bet you anything that for the next ten minutes after you do, you'll conduct an inner monologue of self doubt in your head, where you ask yourself '*Should* I like it?' And, if yes, then '*Why* should I like it?' and 'What's so good about it anyway?'

We seem to have lost our confidence to enquire, or to offer our own opinions or sense of taste around wine. I honestly think this is because of the accepted language we're expected to use; it's too complex and too subjective and we are scared of making mistakes. But, when you're discussing wine, there is simply no definitive answer solely based around flavours and aromas. It's a minefield of endless possibilities and it's no wonder people – even experts at times – can feel uncertain.

SCORES AND MEDALS

Scores, ratings and reviews have become the default benchmark to which many wine drinkers defer when seeking to make an informed decision. This is probably most true for those starting their journey in wine; when you are new to something, it's normal to look to experts in a field. There's also the assumption that scores, reviews and medals are objectively determined by wine experts and wine writers. I won't get into this too much here but

DON'T OVERTHINK IT

Understanding regions, knowing vintages and 'getting' the difference between climate and weather and their influence on wine is important. I'd encourage you to add to your understanding of these as you go. But there is no cookie-cutter approach to wine; as we will see, often the best wines are 'imperfect' in some way and it's what food brings to the mix that actually 'perfects' the taste of those wines. But here, I'm building a broader and (hopefully) more useful picture of wine – without going into the intricacies of regions, vintages and even, in the main, varieties. It's possible to overthink wine, believe me. And overthinking wine is far from what this book – or me, for that matter – is about.

it's worth remembering that our independent print media is diminishing as the online world takes over. More and more, the media is being subverted to meet budgets, with articles increasingly occupying shady areas of advertorial, product placement and marketing. We shouldn't be cynical of all wine writing per se, but it's just good to understand that the ground rules around getting published are shifting. True objectivity, free of agenda, is getting harder to find. It's also worth remembering that wine, and the opinions that swirl around it, are mainly subjective anyway. That's right – much of what you will read about wine is just a subjective opinion. There actually are very few hard and fasts.

To test this theory, here's a practical exercise you can try; I call it 'reviewing the reviewer'. It works like this. Rather than follow a writer because of their fame or perceived expertise, and buying the wines they recommend based on that alone (which many people do), test the reviewer out. Buy some of the wines they recommend highly and if you find you generally like those wines, then follow that writer. If you don't like the wines, then don't follow the writer. It's truly that simple. I don't feel that you need to start – or continue – your wine experience by pinning your sense of enjoyment on what one person thinks. I have seen countless examples where the same wine has been reviewed by three or four different writers, each of them giving different scores and describing the wine quite differently in terms of flavour and aroma. Who is 'right' in this instance? You be the judge.

That is not to say scores are completely redundant when shopping for wine. In some circumstances they are incredibly useful. If you buy a great deal of wine online,

I have seen countless examples where the same wine has been reviewed by three or four different writers, each of them giving different scores and describing the wine quite differently in terms of flavour and aroma.

for example, without the ability to taste or get in-store advice, then scores and ratings can be an invaluable guide. You don't want to fly completely blind. If you are an avid collector of 'museum' (rare) wines, wines with high prices or wines that have significant bottle age, then an expert opinion is a great aid – especially when you're looking for a wine from a vintage that is no longer available through regular channels. Some of these wines can be expensive and you want all the information you can get.

Where scores, ratings and medals don't matter, though, is in restaurants and wine bars. The tasting room, where wines are evaluated and scores and medals dished out, is a sterile place. It's all white coats and long sniffs and endless (and I mean endless) wines to evaluate in a day, a challenge for any palate. In the main there's not a crumb of food to be seen, which means wines are evaluated without any sort of sensory context. They're compared to each other, not considered in conjunction with food – and they're evaluated without any social context either, the very context that gives wine life and meaning. It's a lop-sided process to me. As you will hear me say countless times in this book, I'm as much about the food as I am about the vino. I don't work with wine in isolation from food; there should always be food. Plus it's good to remember that the systems that award medals and such have no over-arching parameters to standardise them. Sometimes points are assigned out of five stars while, other times, it's out of 100 points. The prestige of some wine shows is greater than others, and some have more resources. Some shows are massive and conducted on an international scale, with hundreds or even thousands of wines competing for benchmark awards, while others are way smaller and more localised. When it comes to food and wine, you can't set your clock by wine shows, as there's nothing consistent about how they operate.

I often wonder what the current generation of sommeliers would think about the wines I started working with in my early years on the restaurant floor. Wine hadn't evolved to anywhere near the level of diversity in region, variety and style we see today. Many winemakers around the world pursued the fashion of 'Parker points', named after the influential American wine critic Robert Parker, whose scores out of a possible 100 points became a marketing catchcry for wine producers. If Parker said it, it had to be true. Parker had a predilection for full-throttle red wine fruit bombs from South Australia that were packed with oak, alcohol and weapons-grade levels of fruit sweetness. The fact that these wines were not compatible with food at all was of little concern to him, or anyone else for that matter, such was his status. It was about the final scores and ratings. In Australia, the types of wines this system championed led many wine consumers away from the tastes and textures required for food compatibility, like acidity and tannin, and down the path to high alcohol and gobs of sweetness.

PRICE AND PROMOTION

There is a misconception that if you pay more for a bottle of wine it must taste better than a cheaper one. This perception of 'value' when you buy a wine is where all the wine marketing work is done. The marketing of a wine is

all about what's on the *outside* of a bottle – but none
of that is relevant once you get to the *inside*.

As we have already discussed, a restaurant wine list
reduces all bottles of wine to a consistent font and point
size – on a wine list, all wines look exactly the same, and
the information listed for each is also the same (variety,
region, winemaker or winery, vintage and price). You've
got none of those marketing distractions, such as labels,
medals, product placement or promotions, to sway you.
All you need is some guidance and a trust in your own
preferences and knowledge. In this context, wine finds
its greatest value proposition. The marketing clamour is
stilled and it becomes very much about what's on the
inside of the bottle, not the outside.

I feel the dial has shifted on the customers' idea of
value in wine. Today, increasingly more retail wine
purchases are driven by wine drinkers' experiences in
restaurants and wine bars. It's a reversal of the 1980s and
1990s, when most drinkers would raise an eyebrow at
restaurant prices that were too expensive compared to
the same wine available at half the price in a retail outlet
a few blocks away. Today I find more drinkers are better
informed and not afraid to spend, but are more conscious
of value.

The wine experience

Wine is a dynamic, ever-changing subject and it's hard for
even the best winemaker or the cleverest sommelier to
keep up. There are literally thousands of grape varieties
and tens of thousands of regions, sub-regions and

vineyards all around this planet. It's impossible to get your head around the vast world of wine – believe me, I've tried. The simple truth is that for the majority of your own wine journey, be it a hobby or a lifelong, passionate pursuit, it's the context, attitude, mindset and preferences of the individual that will determine how much a wine is enjoyed, rather than things like flavour and aroma, which are not as important as you might think. By 'mindset' I mean the way we enjoy wine so much more when we are focused on the things around the wine and the context – the food, the people, the vibe and ambience and the occasion – and not just the wine itself. That, for me, is the definition of a 'wine experience'.

Perception of value, the positioning of wines in the market by price point and the enticements of label design – these are all necessary parts of the wine mix, from the outside of the bottle, looking in. But along with florid language about flavour and aroma, these contribute to the confusion around wine – as do scores, critiques, advertising and social media. In fact, these things can actually impede the consideration of wine as simply a liquid in glass – and any attempt to sensibly evaluate whether it's good (or not). The language is not nearly as important as your mindset and the context. There are many things that need to be considered when assessing a wine, and it should never be in isolation. There is the occasion, the season, the people you're with, the location, the food you're eating, the mood and much more.

I realise much of what I'm talking about here is a bit abstract. But stick with me because inevitably you will start to build a sensory vocabulary, through experience and memory, that will open the door on a big, beautiful wine world. The key to unlocking that door comes from learning about mouthfeel, texture, body and balance in wine.

Getting back to basics

To be honest, most of you will know almost instantly whether you like a wine or not, because your sensory faculties instantly register 'yuck' or 'yum' in your brain (see page 87). Where doubts come in, they tend to be driven by ideas and expectations around flavour and aroma in wine, and our own insecurities around our ability to identify and articulate these. I hope you're starting to see that you don't need to get wrapped up in complexities around flavours and aromas to enjoy wine. And this revelation comes as something of a relief. In fact, the idea of trying to understand flavour and aroma before texture and mouthfeel is like attempting to run before you can walk. I can't say this enough. To demonstrate this, imagine for a moment I am selling you a bottle of wine.

I would start by asking you about your taste and preference in wine. I'd want to know if you like the familiar, or if you're prepared to take a punt and go on a bit of an adventure and try something left of field. I'd try to ascertain whether there is a particular grape variety or region that you love. In short, I'd build for us both a picture of your personal taste, without once getting into the terminology around specific flavours or aromas. Such an approach is not designed to answer all your questions

...the idea of trying to understand flavour and aroma before texture and mouthfeel is like attempting to run before you can walk.

around wine; not by a long shot. But what it does achieve is help you build a framework for your own sense of taste and to help define your own, unique relationship with wine in a practical way. Not only will this assist you in finding better value on a wine list and buy better wines at retail, it will also equip you with the confidence to ask all-important questions. And hopefully, it will prompt you to try different wines, so your palate and your tastes can change and grow. It's a 'you-centric' process, not a wine-centric one. If you rush into wine by getting caught up in aroma and flavour, you are entering a highly subjective world, one that will just leave you exhausted by words and choice.

The realisation that you should 'think before you drink' means you also need to start asking the right questions and using the right language. By thinking before you drink I'm making the assumption that you'll drink wine with food. So the thinking should revolve around the following types of questions:

- What sort of food/flavours will you be serving with the wine?
- What is the occasion?
- What is the wine budget?

Using words and ideas that are more in tune with you and your lifestyle makes the process easier and more logical. Starting by defining how you shop, cook, eat, socialise and celebrate occasions, opens up a whole world of possibilities.

A new approach

If we are looking for a more contemporary approach to talking about wine, we need to address the following things: style, drinkability and food compatibility.

STYLE

This relates to the taste and texture of a wine, and this is where the conversation around body, weight, texture and mouthfeel begins. Discussing a wine by its style enables you to articulate what you are looking for on a wine list to a sommelier, or to your local wine retailer. It can also help you create better food matches. The major style categories for wine are as follows (see page 37 for more details on body):

SPARKLING All wines with bubbles, including Champagne
LIGHT-BODIED WHITE Still dry wine
MEDIUM-BODIED WHITE Still dry wine
FULL-BODIED WHITE Still dry wine
ROSÉ (PINK) Still dry wine
LIGHT-BODIED RED Still dry wine
MEDIUM-BODIED RED Still dry wine
FULL-BODIED RED Still dry wine
DESSERT WINE Still sweet wine
FORTIFIED WINE Still sweet wine with increased alcohol levels

DRINKABILITY

This relates to a particular wine's ease of enjoyment; to wines that have a 'more-ish' character; or are what I like to call 'smashable'. A wine's drinkability derives from the right balance between sweetness and dryness. The tension between these two dominant characteristics creates a delicious friction on the palate that leads to an ease of drinking. Importantly, wine with high drinkability leaves your palate fresh and energised. Too much sweetness can clog up your tastebuds, while alcohol, which moonlights as a numbing agent, can desensitise your sense of taste and exhaust your palate. The French call these highly drinkable types of wine, with their fresh and savoury characteristics, *vin de soif* or 'thirsty wine'. They invigorate the palate and make you want to have more. In the same way, a smashable wine is one you can smash back – in an easy-drinking way. More and more, I'm seeing how the market is wanting wines that are clean, crisp, fresh, savoury and elegant, and that pair perfectly with food. I'm also (happily) seeing how the industry is answering by producing more and more of these types of wines.

More and more, I'm seeing how the market is wanting wines that are clean, crisp, fresh, savoury and elegant, and that pair perfectly with food.

FOOD COMPATIBILITY

This relates to how responsive a wine is to food. Sommeliers have a huge role to play in the growth and development of gastronomy, because no other profession is given such a clear remit around that elusive relationship between food and wine – and gastronomy isn't just about food, right? The fact that food is only one half of the gastronomic equation, though, can get lost in translation. When we anticipate a meal at a restaurant, for example, it's not as if we get the same excitement about the wine list as we do about what deliciousness the menu holds. Partly this is exacerbated by the mainstream food media – generally,

It makes perfect sense that if a new generation of chefs is leading the global conversation around food sustainability, then the winemakers who work with them will answer that call, too.

wine lists and wine service struggle to get more than one or two mentions in a restaurant review. They're mostly written about in an 'oh-and-by-the-way' fashion. So it's no wonder the majority of diners place such a low emphasis on wine as part of a restaurant experience.

But nearly every glass of wine you drink in a restaurant you enjoy with food, and the flow-on effects go something like this:

1. You drink a particular wine.
2. You like it.
3. You remember it.
4. You try to find the same thing again, or something close to it, when you want something to drink at home.

So you buy it. All the while, food has played an enormous part in this process. The world of food is opening us up to more types of wines, in that we enjoy a wine that's served with a particular food, and then this sends us off to shop for the wine – especially if you are going to be cooking a similar dish at home. As a result, we have more diversity, quality and food compatibility in wine.

Values

This relates to the importance of the source of a wine and its particular story. It makes perfect sense that if a new generation of chefs is leading the global conversation around food sustainability, then the winemakers who work with them will answer that call, too. A big chunk of the emerging generation of winemakers served their

apprenticeships in large commercial wineries, which, with
their huge teams, budgets and resources, exposed them
to every aspect of the winemaking process.

This isn't unlike chefs who learn their trade in large
classical French kitchens where they're schooled in a broad
range of fundamental techniques, at the highest level of
excellence. Even if those chefs don't hanker to cook French
food when they're qualified, or if they want to run an
informal little bistro with simpler food, that experience
and drilling in the basics is invaluable, equipping them
with a professional value system of the highest level.

So it is with winemakers, who can bring a
sophisticated approach to making even the simplest of
wines, placing them at the pinnacle of emerging trends
around sustainability and ethics, in both cooking and
winemaking. Eschewing commercial 'values' in favour of
emergent ones to do with sustainability, 'whole bunch'
(see page 142), biodynamic or even vegan winemaking
techniques, is becoming important for winemakers and
wine consumers alike.

How you spend your consumption dollars says a lot
about who you are and what your value system is. That
there are winemakers answering the call for transparency
around provenance and origins and making techniques is
heartening for those of us attracted to a more thoughtful
approach to dining and drinking.

BACK STORY AND PROVENANCE
This 'story' aspect is becoming more important in wine, and
it finds clear parallels in where food is at right now. The back

NEW DIVERSITY

As with our personal values, our lifestyle preferences say a lot about how we eat and drink. Do you eat out more than you eat in? Are you a champion home cook who loves to entertain? Are you a staunch vegetarian or do you follow an organic diet? We're surrounded by amazing food options across the gamut and an ever-increasing knowledge around the world of food means an across-the-board increase in ease and confidence around it. Spanish. Thai. Regional Chinese. Sardinian. Vietnamese. Mexican. We're assimilating all kinds of diverse culinary styles into our lives, across the spectrum, from highbrow to cheap and cheerful. How is this translated into wine? The industry is making more wines designed to be drunk young, wines that are less sweet (reflecting the lowering of sugar intake in our diet, and less alcohol as well), and we are also seeing wines of real provenance and quality at price points within our reach. As with the newer value propositions I have mentioned, this is a push back against the overt commercialisation of wine and the assumption that wine can be made just one way. Wine is diverse and unique. We just need to catch up to food in our confidence around wines, learning what we like, when we like it and what we like it with.

story of a piece of produce is really important to diners these days. A good waiter will be able to communicate to you information about a farmer, provenance, growing practices, region, flavour and other bits and pieces that relate to an ingredient, across an entire menu. The story of where something comes from and how it was grown or raised is something we expect to hear, more and more. This lends credibility to a chef, their choice of produce and their cooking.

It's increasingly the same with wine. Wine professionals are embracing the unique narratives around individual wines, where they'd once have expounded on softness, sweetness, fruitiness and such. Now, it's more about the winemaker and their technique, the grapes and the food-friendly qualities of a wine. Insights into the ethos of a winemaker can often say more about the wine than can any taste-based descriptors.

BLIC: balance, length, intensity and complexity

This is a great example of how even the experts use the concepts of texture, taste and mouthfeel. I was speaking to a friend of mine who had recently attempted to attain the Master of Wine, a global qualification that represents the highest level of wine knowledge. MWs are looked upon with awe; it's the absolute pinnacle in wine. During our conversation, we discussed my idea for this book and the notion that it is most useful to think in terms of basic taste, texture and mouthfeel when helping people gain a better understanding of wine. Aroma and flavour are important, but more 'primal' concepts than these actually provide a better entry point to wine. He laughed. 'MWs do that!' he said. 'It's called BLIC, or balance, length, intensity and complexity'.

Even for experts, this BLIC process gives a ready-made framework for assessing a wine, one that involves measuring it as much by structural and tactile characteristics as its particular flavours and aroma. BLIC can help them determine origins, variety and even quality; but it can help you in simpler ways and, importantly, in ways that ultimately lead you back to food. So, let's examine BLIC and what the concepts inherent in it mean for you.

Conceptually, it means that the sum is greater than the parts. So, for example, you wouldn't start with all the flavours in strawberries when planning to cook with them; you'd rather start by considering their acidity and sweetness and you'd take things from there. You wouldn't start with all the fungal notes in mushrooms, but you'd work with their distinctively savoury qualities and build from there. This is exactly the way a chef constructs a dish – it's always simple tastes (and textures) first. Harmony and balance are always key. A chef, for example, doesn't want too much salt in a dish, or bitterness to predominate or for something to be too sweet. Because these would leave a negative impression around the dish, long after it's been eaten. It's all you'll remember – that it was too salty or not sweet enough or overpoweringly acidic. Which leads me to the first component of the BLIC acronym: balance.

BALANCE

Balance in wine is when the tactile and taste components are in harmony. Imagine that alcohol, acidity, tannin and fruit concentration are the pieces of a jigsaw puzzle. On their own, they taste misshapen. When combined, if one or two are in too high a concentration, the result will be awkward and incomplete when tasted. But when all of these pieces come together in a wine in the right proportions, the sensation you get is one of balance. You're not really aware of any of these components individually in the mix. I always think of the legendary

Penfolds Grange when I want a perfect example of balance. Yes, it's a big wine but all elements are equally full, and they balance perfectly.

LENGTH

This is a traditional measure of quality and it refers to the amount of time the flavours of a wine remain in your mouth after you swallow. The longer this period of time, the better the wine. I like using length as a good yardstick for new wine drinkers – if you can still taste a wine a full minute after you've swallowed a mouthful of it, then this is a good indication of flavour concentration and length. Best-quality ripe fruit will have an incredibly intense flavour and better 'length', like a tree-ripened apricot versus a pallid, unripe, cool-stored one. It articulates the connection between fruit concentration and a wine's acidity and tannin, which are its frameworks. Fruit concentration can get stuck at the front of your palate if it's in excess (that is, if a wine has too much sweetness). Acidity and tannin draw the flavours of the wine towards the back of your palate, where they exert a 'stretching' impact on the mouthfeel and the weight of the wine. In this way, they make it feel longer in shape and in length of flavour in your mouth.

INTENSITY

This refers to the colour and aroma of a wine. Colour is not just about measuring pigment but also the depth of the colour, and the clarity of it. It's important to note that orange and amber wines challenge convention here. Ask about the wine's appearance before ordering it to recalibrate; if it's a little cloudy don't fret (see page 140). Intensity of aroma points to both the power of the aromas and the quality of the aromas themselves. Think of measuring intensity in terms of it being represented on an old-fashioned volume dial, like on a radio, with the notches cycling up from 1 through to 10. On the dial, 1 is the lowest intensity and 10 the highest. To apply the same measure to heat in food, 1 would be watery and 10 would represent biting into a raw chilli. With wine intensity, I'd rate a pinot noir at an 8 in aromatic intensity. A cabernet sauvignon I'd clock in at 8 ½ in tannin intensity, 8 in fruit intensity and 7 in acid intensity. To a riesling I'd give 9 in acid intensity and 3 in sweetness and 0 in tannin. Wines that have low intensity across the entire spectrum are quite simply not good wines.

COMPLEXITY

Complexity is a character in wine that you need to go looking for. It won't pop up in low-priced, easy-drinking, mass-produced wines. Complexity is rooted in the soil, in the vine, in good winemaking technique and often, but not always, in bottle age. Generally wines that are produced with a 'small wine' making philosophy (see page 151), end up being more reflective of their region and vineyard/s than do cheaper, mass-produced wines. More commercial wines are made with consistency in mind, whereas in a more complex wine, idiosyncrasies and quirks, which lend complexity, are encouraged.

Parallels in wine and food

Body, texture and mouthfeel are not only the fundamentals of wine, they're also fundamental to good cooking. It helps to understand wine better if we consider food, and learn a little about some similarities in the approaches to making food and making wine.

One of my greatest mentors was French-born chef Guillaume Brahimi. A product of three Michelin-starred brigade kitchens in Paris, and iconic chef Joël Robuchon's Jamin restaurant; 'GB' could be terrifying and inspiring all at the same time. He was obsessed with the drive for perfection in the produce, preparation and execution behind a menu.

Classical French cuisine is still the benchmark for gastronomy the world over. Its techniques and sensibilities are what the fundamentals of good cooking are rooted in. For a chef to get the right perspective on cooking, they go through a rounded and rigorous training in basics, which later gives them the ability to experiment and maybe even break rules. Mastering techniques like braising, poaching and frying, learning competent knife skills and knowing how to build flavours in a dish, understanding how to make a good stock, and so on; these are all vital elements in a chef's learning. Maybe they never end up making the ultimate pâté or soufflé, or perhaps they're not interested in replicating classical sauces, but they know all the appropriate techniques anyway, and they understand how to apply them elsewhere.

It's the same with a winemaker. Good ones are steeped in hardcore basics, across the spectrum of techniques and business. So when they run off and get into 'whole bunch' winemaking (see page 142) or specialise in, say, mouthwatering pétillant naturel wines (see page 135), they're coming from a place of knowing the basics. They're not just trotting off on some blind tangent.

What I'm trying to demonstrate is, that even if you're confronted with an entirely new style of wine, you can still revert, as does the winemaker, to the basics when trying to come to terms with it. The basics remain as a background constant in wine, as they do in cooking. We have restaurant dishes today that reflect the voice of a whole new generation of cooks, unheard of in previous decades. But in them you can still identify the threads of classical cooking, and they still have to succeed at the coal face of customer expectations – these dishes simply have to TASTE good. It's the same with wine.

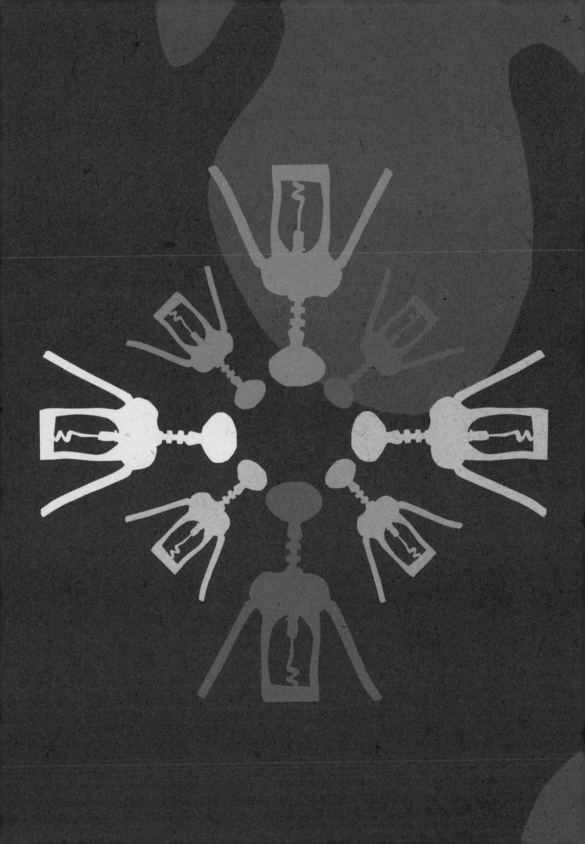

A MATTER OF TASTE

WINE NOTE

I have to maintain some form of objectivity in my work because, as we've already seen, that work is not at all about me and I have to cater to different tastes. I need to be 'across' wine in a knowledge-based way so I can maintain some semblance of objectivity. I don't particularly enjoy oaked wines, for example, but I still need to have a thorough appreciation of them, because plenty of others do like them. But the truth is, there is now so much more diversity in wines (varieties, techniques, regions) than ever before, that reductive scoring and a boxed-in approach around varieties aren't very relevant to the everyday wine drinker's relationship with wine, particularly in a restaurant or dining situation.

It's time for a bit of reprogramming around the 'technical' assessment of wine, particularly in regard to taste. Now, a formal, technical approach is a valuable tool for the wine professional, giving them the ability to assess wines according to a recognised form of benchmarking. Professionals understand the entire journey of wine from vineyard to bottle – where it was grown, the year it was made, what it was made from and how this impacts on the finished wine. All of this is well and good, but I'm here to reassure you that drinking wine is not about putting it through a test, and that it isn't necessary to grasp the entire technical backstory in order to know and enjoy wine. There is, of course, a certain methodology you have to adhere to if you're being paid as a wine professional, but this chapter is all about a new approach to 'taste'. It is designed to help you appreciate wine in a more personal, contemporary, user-friendly way rather than thinking you have to turn to rigid doctrines, processes and systems.

It's also about equipping you with a simpler 'tasting toolkit' than the one traditionally based around flavour and aroma and the myriad subjective and, often confusing, descriptors used by wine professionals, so you can establish a sense of confidence in your own sense of wine taste. There are basics to grasp, but these are not as complex as you might think. You honestly don't need to get tangled up in technology, science or technical 'wine speak' to understand wine. In fact, it's far better if you don't.

It's actually OK to go with your gut. That's really what this book is fundamentally about; the idea that your first impressions of a wine do count and all you need is the confidence to go with these. There are some abstract ideas in what I'm about to say. I'm not providing you with a prescriptive approach, nor any hard and fast rules. Rather, what I'm imparting is as much about the individual and the personal tastes of you, the wine drinker, as it is about a certain wine. Many of you already have the beginnings of a tasting toolkit, and you find these in the statements you make, such as, 'I like dry wine' or, 'I like fruity wines', or, 'I don't like oak'. Most of us have these opinions about wine at least and, in them, you're halfway there.

In this chapter, what we will consider are the basic tastes that make up both wine and food, and how you can use these to crack onto simple but effective pairings. We'll look at ideas around body, texture and mouthfeel, and the way these aspects help you approach the idea of matching wine to food in a simpler, more tactile way.

Tasting wine is a very different proposition from *drinking* wine; the former is to do with pure evaluation and the latter with enjoyment.

Traditional tasting techniques

There is an important place for a sound *tasting* technique, but really it belongs with the professionals and I'd urge you to leave it there. *Tasting* wine is a very different proposition from *drinking* wine; the former is to do with pure evaluation and the latter with enjoyment.

Let's talk for a moment, though about tasting, or evaluating, wines so you can better understand the distinction. Tasting wines should be done according to a consistent process or system because this results, in theory, in objectivity and impartiality. I remember talking with legendary Australian wine writer James Halliday many years ago at a wine show in Sydney. He said to me, in a quiet moment between judging sessions, that a wine could cost $5 or $500, it could be artisanal and hand-crafted or it could be from a high-volume commercial winery. But regardless of its pedigree, he believed every wine deserves equal treatment in regards to the tasting approach. Having a good tasting technique gives the pro a methodology that makes it possible to dissect a wine down to its finest detail. This more structured kind of evaluation enables you to break down a wine and measure its qualities across multiple criteria. As I mentioned in the Old rules, new thinking chapter, tasting rooms are generally sterile spaces, devoid of smell and noise. Wines are tasted without food – introducing a food element into the mix jeopardises accuracy and consistency because, as we're learning, food changes wine. You will have realised by now that none of this technical stuff is what this book is about. The idea of wine as an overall 'experience' depends on too many other elements and ones that are too good to leave out. The object for us here is to find the right wine to fit the occasion, the company and the food that are important to us.

However, there are two things professionals do when tasting that are actually really helpful.

1. SWIRLING A WINE

Swirling wine in a glass isn't pretentious; there's actually a cool bit of science at work here. Any liquid kept in a confined area is subject to the creation of surface tension, which effectively forms a cap over the surface. With wine, this prevents aroma being released. By swirling, you disturb that cap, agitating and aerating the wine, which opens it up.

The best swirling technique is as follows. Put your glass of wine on the table. Now put your index finger on one side of the base of the stem and your middle finger on the other side, then swirl the glass in a smooth, circular motion, keeping the base of the glass on the table. I believe that swirling is really important; before you drink you should definitely swirl.

2. SPITTING WINE

Despite my profession, I'm actually not a big drinker. So I learned to spit – rather effectively, if I say so myself – very early in my career. When I'm judging wines, I can sample hundreds in a day; I need my head clear, and spitting becomes essential.

If you are trying a lot of wines at cellar doors or some retail event, spitting is also necessary. I taught myself good technique by practising every time I cleaned my teeth. You need to form the liquid in your mouth into a 'ball' then quickly force it out between pursed lips. I now have a sniper-rifle spit – I can hit a bucket six feet away. As well as being a highly practical skill, nothing makes you appear more proficient in wine than having good spitting prowess, believe me.

Three important things to consider

An easier way 'in' to wine than through the tasting room can be found in the following three ideas. Remember these when you're tasting a wine for the first time – whether in a vineyard, a cellar door, retail outlet, restaurant or in your own home – and let them be an overarching foundation for you.

Tastings were
focused on a
'glass backwards'
approach, where
the objective was
to 'unsee' all the
marketing, branding
and pricing,
and consider a
wine free of the
preconceptions
these can introduce.

1. WHERE ARE YOU, WHO ARE YOU WITH, AND WHY?

Your surroundings have a big impact on how much you appreciate a particular wine. Are you outside? Is it warm or cold? Are you at a party or other special occasion? Are you in your favourite restaurant or at home cooking for friends? Not only does the setting and occasion affect the way you taste a wine but it also changes your opinion on which wines you think are suitable in the first place. For example, let's take prosecco. It's best served chilled, when it's bubbly. Its refreshing qualities are the perfect antidote to the warmth of a summer's afternoon. Now, picture that same frosty glass of prosecco on a chilly winter night. You're sitting by the fire and the comforting aromas of meat roasting for dinner are wafting about. It just doesn't fit, does it? Always consider your surroundings when drinking a wine; one size never fits all. Another consideration is who you are with. You rarely order a wine just to satisfy yourself. Ask the people you are with what they generally prefer to drink; always consider the needs of the company you are in when ordering or opening wine. Taking care of others first should be at the heart of sharing wine.

2. PICTURE YOUR WINE NAKED

In my various roles as a group sommelier or wine director, I had to set up tasting panels in order to formally evaluate wines. Attendees were nominated by the restaurant managers and everyone who participated had an equal vote; we literally sat around a table. Tastings were focused on a 'glass backwards' approach, where the objective was to 'unsee' all the marketing, branding and pricing, and consider a wine free of the preconceptions these can introduce. There were no tasting notes or reviews to reference. All we had was a copy of the restaurant's current menu and the wine list. The object was to maintain a purely egalitarian approach to a wine – it didn't matter if it was red burgundy or some cheeky cheap-and-cheerful, at the end of the day it was all liquid in a glass, regardless of pedigree or price. They were all treated the same. We would taste a wine, considering its structure, balance and mouthfeel. We would then discuss food and which dishes from the current menu would match. Often, some of the key chefs would attend the panels, to give extra insight into the menu and discuss what they were planning to put on it next. We would then start to talk about the region, variety and the wine's particular story. In all of this, our aim was to remove all the marketing from the mix and consider a wine as a guest in a restaurant would. As a wine in a glass. Naked.

3. FIRST IMPRESSIONS – YUCK OR YUM?

In the end, this is what it comes down to. I like this or I don't like it. It's either 'yuck' or 'yum'. First impressions are vitally important and often they're the most accurate ones, too. Some wines will surprise you, revealing their true potential with time in a glass or decanter. But in the final analysis, wine is a personal and subjective experience, and generally your first moments with it will tell you volumes. It's OK for your opinion of the wine to be different from someone else's. What's important is to be able to articulate why. This is how your palate and knowledge can really develop, and your confidence can be boosted.

The difference between taste and flavour

How are flavour and taste different and why is this important? The common cold can help us understand how. A cold, incurable and annoying, has symptoms such as a bunged up nasal passage – and we all know how aggravating it is to not be able to taste food properly when your nose is blocked. The reason for this is because aroma can't travel from your palate to your nose – it's those aromas that your nose captures that help you experience flavour, rather than just one of the five basic tastes. Your tongue simply registers the five basic 'tastes' and that's all.

Place the tip of a finger on the skin above your nose and between your eyebrows. Under the skin here is the olfactory nerve. It has thousands of little sensors that detect aromas that the brain translates into flavour. Truly, your nose is incredible. And it is so vital in recognising flavours in wine as well as in food. For example, if you eat a piece of chocolate when you have a cold, your tongue will only register the taste 'sweet'; you won't get any complex chocolate flavours at all, as your nose is out of action. In this instance, you could've eaten a handful of sugar, as far as your mouth is concerned. Your palate can only detect and measure the concentrations of the five basic tastes:

1. SOUR
2. SWEET
3. SALT
4. BITTER
5. UMAMI

Both food and wine have different concentrations of the five basic tastes, and these register on your tongue. The idea behind successful food- and wine-pairing is to build an outline of a dish, based on which of the five tastes it contains, as well as the textures, then match those to the corresponding characters in a wine. Certain combinations of tastes in one are complementary to the tastes in the other. When considering a dish, we are looking to identify just one or two simple elements. For example, in Mediterranean dishes you'll readily identify salt and oil (which can register as slightly acid and slightly oily or fatty). Every dish will exhibit a balance of at least a couple of flavours, and these give the diner the impression of tastes across the salty, acid, sweet, bitter and umami spectrum.

Entire cuisines are built on readily identified tastes. In Chinese cuisine, for example, salt, umami and sour reign supreme. Think of Thai cooking, a cuisine marked by the balance of hot, salty, sour and sweet flavours. What these give you is an overall impression of a dish, long after you've eaten it, which can be distilled down to a general statement – for example, 'That dish was fresh, clean and delicate' or, 'That stew tasted robust, savoury and rich'. You don't tend to recall an entire list of ingredients – just the overwhelming impression. And it's these threads you are looking for in an accompanying wine. The food and wine need to meet in the 'middle' of these threads – that place where they complement each other on the taste and flavour (and texture) spectrum.

The five basic tastes are put into a completely different context when wine is in the equation, as mixing wine with food can change tastes, perhaps softening their effects or maybe even accentuating them. Remember, though, that everyone's palate is different, and your palate can even shift over the years from one preference (sweet, for example) to another (savoury). One person may also register bitterness, or acidity or sweetness more strongly than another person might. So bear this in mind because, as always, there are few hard and fasts.

To illustrate this, I'll share with you a quick story. A few years ago I was in Logroño in the Rioja region of Spain. I was there for work as a wine ambassador, but my trip coincided with an annual festival. The whole town was on the street, partying. I noticed lots of people, including the well-respected local winemakers, carrying pig-skin bladders filled with wine and they were knocking the contents back. Everyone was having a fantastic time, and I assumed the contents of those bladders was something pretty special, given my location in the wine world. As it turned out, those bladders were filled with local red wine ... mixed with Coca-Cola. I was a bit taken aback but decided to try it and,

TASTING FOOD AND WINE TOGETHER

If you are tasting food and wine together, you should try to eat some food first, then try your wine. Those first impressions of the meal will connect with your first impressions of the wine, creating the active space where food- and wine-matching comes to life.

I have to say, that combo tasted pretty good. The sweet fizziness went well with the fun, festive atmosphere, but there was something else happening as well. The local reds are high in tannins, and the sugar in the Coke smashed them, making the wine more-ish and easy to drink.

In this same way, you'll see more and more how the basic tastes in wine can be modified and changed by introducing foods that complement or even smooth out wrinkly aspects of it. And vice versa. The introduction of a wine can affect flavour and texture in foods by minimising them, accentuating them or harmonising with them. As a side note, that event in Spain also taught me not to be TOO serious about wine. Sometimes, it's OK to just have some fun with it. Please don't be too purist!)

Wine, food and the five basic tastes

The five basic tastes all play an important role in wine. However, they may make an appearance under another term, more apt for describing the traits of wine – for example, sourness is generally referred to as 'acidity' in relation to wine. And, of course, there can be huge variations in the spectrum of each taste, depending on many other influencing factors, from food to the occasion, as I discuss throughout this book. When it comes to wine, you can't really consider any one factor in isolation. Have you ever wondered why natural oysters are served with vinaigrette or why fish and chips taste better with lemon and salt? These are all everyday examples of how the basic tastes work together, and the same principles apply to matching wine and food.

SOUR

Sourness in wine relates to 'acidity'. This is a taste that gives wine sharp, sour characters. Acidity helps activate your appetite, which is why aperitifs are always dry and acid. It also gets your gustatory instincts going. This process is where the term 'mouthwatering' comes from – acids in food and wine literally kick your salivary glands into top gear. To better understand the taste of acidity, drink water to neutralise your palate, then immediately bite into a wedge of lemon. That distinctive mouth-puckering sensation you get is the effect of acidity.

SWEET

Sweetness is a soft, cloying sensation that feels smooth and supple on the palate. Sweetness in food will accentuate any acidity in wine, making it taste 'hard' or overly acidic. For this reason, when matching food sweetness with wine sweetness, I always try to make the wine sweetness a touch higher than that of the food. Don't get confused between sweetness and fruitiness – there is a difference. 'Sweet' refers to the taste commonly associated with sugar, the kind you typically find in dessert-style wines. 'Fruitiness', or fruit concentration, is related to the level of fruit flavour in wine. I have lost count of how many customers have asked me for a 'sweet' wine when all they wanted was a dry wine with lots of fruit flavour. Unless specified in a wine list under a different category, such as dessert, fortified or sweet, any wine listed is considered 'dry'. Remember, if you ask for a 'sweet' wine you will be served a dessert wine or a wine with strongly perceptible levels of sweetness.

CARAMELISING

Caramelising adds both a savoury and a sweet note to food, and results from cooking techniques like roasting, frying or grilling (see Cooking techniques, page 113).Caramelising (searing) food is the result of the sugar and proteins in food coming into direct contact with heat. It's that sticky stuff left in a frying pan after you have cooked bacon until it's crispy, or the carpet of brownish black left in the tin after you have roasted a leg of lamb.

SALT

In food and wine matching, the salt is largely drawn from the food and cooking. In the interests of full disclosure, I have to say I am a salt freak. I love saltiness in all its forms, from the delicate tang of an oyster to the piercing saline taste of anchovies. While I love saltiness, it's not a taste you generally get in wine. Salt is largely a food-based taste.

However, salt in food plays an important role with certain types of wine. Salt works wonders with acidity, but it can harden tannins and make them seem more bitter. I love working with salt because it can also be added to food at your discretion, which gives you more control over the food- and wine-matching process.

Always remember, though, that a lot of produce will have high salt levels, so be careful when adding salt to food or when cooking. There is a fine line between 'seasoning' a dish and having it taste too salty.

BITTER

I love bitterness. While it's another taste more common in food, bitterness can also be detected in wine in the form of tannins. Tannins tackle fatty foods and can clean the palate in much the same way that acidity does. If you want to learn about bitterness in wine and what it feels like, cleanse your mouth with water, then taste strong, cold, black tea, which is super high in tannin. A basic rule of thumb I use for bitterness in food and wine matching is: the more texture in the protein and the higher the fat content, the better bitterness can work.

UMAMI

This taste is the sommelier's best friend. Umami is a Japanese word that loosely translates as 'a pleasant savoury taste'. As an Australian, I grew up with umami in the form of Vegemite, a savoury yeast spread similar to British Marmite. Umami is the taste behind a good stock, and it's also that more-ish factor in cheese. If you want to learn about umami, just bite into a chunk of really good-quality parmesan.

Techniques such as fermenting, curing and ageing all help release more umami tastes from vegetables and meats. This has been known for a long time – the ancient Greeks and Romans made an umami-laden fermented fish sauce known as 'garum' to flavour their food. Traditional Asian soy, fish and oyster sauces are also classic examples of the umami flavour. Foods high in certain types of glutamate are rich in umami, such as, fish, shellfish, mushrooms and many ripe vegetables. It is also found in dishes based on slow and steady cooking, especially ones where red meats are involved. Umami's taste profile is loosely savoury and it works well with wines that show a pronounced acidity, are low in alcohol and have a bit of freshness. If the food you're working with is salty, a little sweetness is appropriate in your wine – but not too much. White wines with oxidative characters (including dry sherry and skin-contact wines – orange and amber wines – see page 140) have a real affinity with umami tastes.

A few other key tastes

Apart from these essential five tastes, here are some more that I consider essential to this discussion. They also happen to be tastes that I really like working with.

SAVOURY

Essentially, savoury foods are not sweet ones. Savoury is the quality in food that sets your mouth on edge in a good way, making you salivate and reach for a bottle of wine. As we move away from a diet driven by sugar, savoury tastes are becoming more popular. Overall, restaurant menus are lightening up. There's less heavy saucing, fewer heavy carbs, and vegetables are more often becoming the 'hero' of a menu, not just presented as an accompaniment or an afterthought. Most importantly, savoury flavours now extend across the whole menu – they can even appear in cocktails and desserts these days. Some foods are inherently more savoury than others – fried mushrooms, a meaty braise or a good, cheesy risotto are all deeply savoury. In this, savoury intersects with umami to a large

Heavy, buttery sauces aren't the thing they once were — but neither is the neurotic trimming and discarding of fat from, say, a pork belly roast.

extent (see Umami, page 94). Savoury dishes are largely defined as those that lean towards more salt and spice than sweetness. It's a large, amorphous group that occurs across all courses, seasons, textures and weights.

FAT

More of us are embracing fat. For the longest time, it's been vilified and pronounced 'unhealthy', but science now tells us this isn't entirely true, as there are 'good' and 'bad' fats. Chefs have always employed fats in their cooking. For them, butter and oil are indispensable; they add richness, softness, a melting texture and unbelievable mouthfeel to dishes. Fat in meat, such as the marbling in a steak or roast, melts through the flesh as it cooks, giving a wonderful juiciness and incredible depth of flavour. Fats in fish are different; they are far more delicate and many are concentrated right under the skin or in the belly. Some fish are oilier than others – tuna, salmon and swordfish, for example, are way oilier than white fish like snapper or bream.

Good modern cooking enhances the fats already present without adding ridiculous extra amounts, as was done in the past. Heavy, buttery sauces aren't the thing they once were – but neither is the neurotic trimming and discarding of fat from, say, a pork belly roast. It's good news for food lovers that natural fats are having a bit of a renaissance.

When considering fats in food, look to wines that have medium to high levels of acidity and similar levels of tannin and fruit concentration (see Fat and 'cut', page 101).

PICKLING

Pickled vegetables are de rigueur today; just look at any contemporary restaurant menu. Pickles rely on vinegar and salt (and sometimes sugar) as these two things are preservatives (as is sugar) in high concentrations. But they make for a tough wine-matching proposition as a pickle is essentially an acid bomb on the palate. For that reason, most pickled dishes are presented at the beginning of a menu. If they are included in a dish, they are usually there to balance a rich or fatty element or enhance a delicate, subtle one. (A match will also depend on any herbs or spices used, as these tend to be strongly flavoured ones, but always start by focusing on texture and the basic tastes.)

When finding wines to go with pickles, look to those with high acidity, good intensity of fruit flavour and no, and I mean NO, oak. Sparkling wine, manzanilla sherry and rosé – the pale, light-bodied, crisp and fruity iterations – fit well, as does riesling, particularly the slightly refreshingly sweet versions from Germany. (See also Acid and acid, page 100.)

SMOKE

Smoking is another ancient food preservation technique now used widely for the aroma, flavour and texture it brings to certain foods. Hot smoking acts like a sealant with proteins like meat and fish; their flesh will be moist and the flavours most potent. Smoky flavours can also come from cooking over coals or wood, as well as from the physical smoking of foods. And those smoke-infused 'black bits', which come from the charring of meats over fire, are great to work with in wine matching.

When looking for a wine to go with smoky foods, whether smoke- or fire-cooked, you should take into account the level of smoking in the dish. Lightly smoked seafoods, like mussels or oysters, will require wines with freshness and increased texture. If there's more smoke in the food, look to dial up the oak character of your wine. A barbecue will lend smokiness to whatever you cook on it (chicken, vegetables, sausages, steak), and for all of these you need wines that are medium- to full-bodied and richly fruited with firm tannins and some oak character. To match foods cooked on the barbecue, try zinfandel, dolcetto, barbera, agiorgitiko and mencía, and red blends of grenache, shiraz and mourvèdre.

FERMENTING

Like smoking and pickling, the fermenting of food has gone well beyond storage and preservation necessities (as they once were), to become integral to mainstream menu planning. Light-bodied, un-oaked white wines with a little sweetness have a history with fermenting. The delicious spätlese and auslese rieslings of Germany, for example, are the traditional wine to have with sauerkraut, or fermented cabbage. Nowadays we all seem to love Korean kimchi, another triumph of fermentation, and light-bodied, crisp, crunchy red wines, rippling with acidity, go perfectly with its potent spice. The common denominator with fermented foods is to avoid fuller bodied wines that have higher levels of oak character or tannins.

HEAT

The important thing here is to note the difference between 'spice' and 'heat'. Spice is where there is a potency in aroma, and is derived from warm, dry spices like pepper, cinnamon, ginger and nutmeg. But heat is that fiery sensation that can either tickle or sting the palate, depending on its intensity, and it comes, of course, from chilli. It's a palpable sensation that can cause momentary discomfort in your mouth and make you sweat. But it can also elevate and enrich the flavours of food. You'll mainly find this kind of heat in Southeast Asian, Chinese and Mexican cooking, although Indian food can be hot, as well as very spicy and complex.

Wine has a temperamental, if not difficult, relationship with heat. Definitely avoid wines with high alcohol, oak or tannin. Look for wines that are light- to medium-bodied, with little or no oak and with a softer texture and sweeter edge. Acidity also plays a role here, as whites that have some 'refreshing' qualities alongside their sweetness work well with heat. What this means is not that they taste overtly 'sweet' per se, but that they have a perky fruit ripeness and aroma that's well balanced by acidity. Whites to look for are sparkling wines, riesling (a little sweet), fiano, gewürztraminer, pinot gris and sauvignon blanc. Good reds would be pinot noir, gamay, grenache and merlot.

Quick-reference tasting toolkit

Planning food and wine matches requires a few basic tools, namely a collection of 'one–two' combinations that will help you find the right wine for the food, occasion and company. Learning these tools can give you so much more confidence when a wine list and menu are thrust into your hands, or when you are planning a dinner party at home. As a sommelier I have developed my own quick reference 'toolkit' of basic taste and texture combinations. My toolkit helps me develop a constructive dialogue with the chef, allows me to pick the right wine for the food and provides me with a clear description of, and reasoning behind, the pairing. On the following pages is my toolkit. These vital principles will help you understand the process of food and wine matching in a restaurant or in your own home.

ACID AND ACID

Acid can be used in many ways. I love working with foods that have high acidity, putting them with wines that are

ACID AND SWEET

While high-acid wines work well with salt and fat, the same can't be said for sweetness. Imagine biting into a milk chocolate bar full of sweet, warming, cloying and unctuous textures and taste. Now imagine biting into a green apple, tart and sour with a tangy and fresh flavour. I bet your face twisted just thinking about this scenario. It's twisting because of the way sweetness would amplify the acidity, making the whole combination coarse, hard and unpleasant. In a wine, acidity and sweetness are vital and complementary components (see Dessert wine, page 37). One keeps the other in check.
With food and wine I rarely go here.

equally acidic in nature. If a cheese has high natural acidity (like those made from goat's milk, for example), then a high-acid wine such as a fresh, crisp sauvignon blanc – especially one from the Sancerre region of France – is the best partner.

ACID AND SALT

Hot chips (fries), which are all about fat and salt, go brilliantly with sparkling white wines that show strips of acidity. Acid counterbalances salt, but it cuts through fat as well (see Fat and 'cut' below). Think of a squeeze of lemon over battered, deep-fried fish, seasoned with a bit of salt, and you'll see what I mean. Creamy, salty oysters are fantastic with acidic white wines. What you get in these examples is a basic equation of acidity + fat + salt at work and it's a magic, fail-safe combo. Plus, in this scenario, the wine's mouthfeel will change; it will become rounder and appear fruitier. Also try salty, cured meats like prosciutto with high-acid reds like pinot noir.

FAT AND 'CUT'

Fat carries flavours in food, but isn't a flavour itself – it's just a vehicle. Fat in food gives an unctuous, warming, enriching note. Cutting fats is the job of acidity and tannin in wine. Chefs work with different kinds of fat – butter, olive oil and lard, for example – and each type needs the acid in wine to 'cut' the fat in your mouth. Essentially, fat in food can build up in your mouth and literally clog your tastebuds. Acidity and tannin act like a windshield wiper that swooshes across the tongue, stripping out the fat and rebooting your palate. Acid and tannin lift the flavours and minimise the sensation of fat in your mouth. When a wine is described as being 'refreshing', this refers to the sensation you get when acidity and tannin clean out the fats around your tastebuds.

Remember, all wine has some level of acidity, but tannin is mainly found in red wine. How much you need, whether the wine is light-, medium- or full-bodied and what colour it is, comes down to the level of fat in the dish. And the overall weight and texture of the dish also needs to be considered. For example, smoked salmon, which is fatty but cold, salty and light, will require a different wine from a hunk of rare roast beef rib-eye. Go for white wines like riesling, pinot gris, chenin blanc or skin contact-rich white for pink-fleshed fish. These will soak up fat and oil like a sponge. Reds can be gamay, pinot noir, nebbiolo, sangiovese, malbec, tempranillo, rosso di montalcino, mourvèdre, cool-climate shiraz (syrah), or something quirky like nerello mascalese.

PROTEIN AND 'GRIP'

The drying sensation in your mouth that you experience when you drink a wine is caused by tannins (see page 41). The reason your mouth dries out is because your saliva is largely made up of protein molecules and, when tannins in wine come into contact with saliva, those tannins run straight to the salivary glands at the back of your palate, literally sucking them dry. And when protein and tannin combine, the tannins will drop out of the wine and the texture suddenly softens, revealing more of the wine's fruit character. The rule with tannins is to ensure that the concentration of them in the wine matches the intensity of the fat and protein in the food. Essentially, you need protein to soften tannins. The 'bigger' the tannins in the wine, the bigger and more dense the proteins need to be. In food, those proteins will taste almost sweeter and more flavoursome.

One of the words I love to use when discussing food and wine together is 'grip'. This refers to the level of tannin in a wine – the more tannin, the greater the grip. Big pieces of protein work with wines that have a lot of grip – wines like cabernet sauvignon, malbec, mataro or shiraz, for example. (Try a rib-eye steak with a high-tannin red wine from the Rioja region in Spain.) Smaller pieces of protein need wines with less grip, such as gamay, pinot noir, nebbiolo and grenache. Skin-contact white wines (see page 139) will carry some astringency and bitterness. Drink them with fatty white proteins like pork or roast chicken and the bitterness will slip away, making the wine fresher and more flavoursome.

OAK AND LACTIC

Lactic flavours, such as those derived from butter and cream, are super with wines made with, or stored in, oak. Working in French kitchens for so long, I learned to appreciate the way butter can be used as an accepted flavour enhancer. A good portion of the full-bodied white category on any wine list I oversaw, leaned towards a style enriched with the creamy textures and buttery mouthfeel you get from contact with oak.

One of the words I love to use when discussing food and wine together is 'grip'. This refers to the level of tannin in a wine – the more tannin, the greater the grip.

SWEET AND HEAT

Growing up in Australia, a country where the smells and flavours of Thai cuisine are so popular, meant finding wines for food infused with chilli-heat and spice. Hot food is famously difficult with full-bodied wines, as tannins in particular will magnify the effect of heat in food. Light-bodied wines are best. With fragrant, spicy dishes, white wines with a touch of sweetness can reduce the perception of heat. Likewise, rich red protein-based dishes like beef or lamb curries suit light-bodied, fruity reds.

SALT AND SWEET

Sweet is attractive with salty flavours – think of salted caramel, for example. I see the combination of sweet and salt used a great deal in food. Sweetness in wine will enhance saltiness in food – for example, we know how melon accentuates the salty, savoury characteristics of prosciutto. And seriously, who doesn't love maple syrup with bacon, or Balinese black sticky rice, sweet but spiked with a perceptible dose of salt? Salt (fish sauce) with sweet (mirin in Japanese cooking, or palm sugar/jaggery in Thai) are the heart and soul of the more-ish sauces used in Pan Asian cooking. A fruity riesling with a Thai or Vietnamese dish with fish sauce is fantastic.

For savoury courses I like to use acidity to counterbalance salt, as the acid promotes freshness. White wines with a refreshing sweetness can be used as long as they are not cloying or 'sugary'. Start off using sweetness in wine with cheese. The creamy, salty, nature of blue cheese suits a 'sweetish' riesling, such as a spätlese (made with 'late-

USE FAMILIAR TERMS

By thinking about the way you talk about food, you can develop a simpler, clearer wine language. This language can strip back and articulate wine using words and terms that you associate with food. These are words that focus more on texture, balance and the marriage of basic taste rather than any personal belief systems and subjectivity. Use words like supple, crisp, rich, savoury, fresh and vibrant.

picked' grapes) or auslese (made with 'out-picked', or specially selected, grapes). Also, blue cheese with port is a classic salt and sweet combination.

SWEET AND SWEET

This is a 'gimme' for most diners. At the end of the meal, especially a long one full of salty, savoury food, your body is crying out for sugar – primarily as a way to jump-start your metabolism to start processing the food you have just eaten. Sweet foods tend to love sweet wines. A good sweet food with sweet wine match is chocolate cake and a fortified wine like muscat. However, I have one golden rule when matching sweet dishes with sweet wines. The wine must be less sweet than the food. Most great dessert-style wines are defined by their acidity and freshness, not by their sweetness. When choosing wine, always ask about the levels of acidity as well as sweetness.

SAVOURY AND SAVOURY

From a wine perspective, savouriness is my favourite character in food to work with. It's generally found in foods with a salty or spicy character that aren't overly sweet. If you take the weight and texture of food with savoury characteristics, then you are automatically looking for light- to medium-bodied wines with delicate, sweet fruit flavours, little oak but with soft and savoury tannins. Wines partnered with savoury dishes should linger in the medium-bodied spectrum. They should be wines that are versatile and that literally 'shape shift' when you get the balance between texture and basic taste right. Avoid wines with high tannins, oak levels and alcohol. Wines with soft tannins and relatively high acidity work best. Remember when you taste the wines to make sure that behind all that acid and tannin there sits a good level of fruit character. Wines with an oxidised character work well, too, as they carry high levels of umami, which is great with savoury food.

Trust your gut

Learning about how basic tastes work in food and wine helps your wine vocabulary, but also gives you insights into the mindset and language of a chef. If you are a sommelier, then there is a good chance that nine out of ten glasses of wine that you will sell and serve will be served with food. However, for the diner, the idea of wine and food together is a custom they may observe only on special occasions. A customer might choose the degustation menu with specifically matched wines, or just want a good bottle of red with their steak. It really comes down to personal taste.

The tasting toolkit in this chapter is about giving the diner, home entertainer and wine drinker insights into the techniques that I use when drinking, enjoying and, ultimately, evaluating a glass of wine. A great deal of what we love in wine and food comes from our 'gut'. Trusting these feelings and learning to embrace the things that go with wine – like food, occasion and company – will not only help you unlock more enjoyment from wine, but will make you a far better student of wine as well.

MATCHING FOOD
AND WINE

WINE NOTE

Although I've spent the majority of my career serving wine on restaurant floors, my best memories of this work are actually not from the cellar or the tasting table, but from the kitchen. The discussions and debates I've had with great chefs around food and wine are the work memories I ultimately cherish; they're the ones that have guided me most closely over my years in service. I still get a real kick out of watching a brigade of 20 or so chefs during a Saturday dinner service, when, with backs against the wall, they scream in unison, 'YES CHEF!' I never get tired of seeing this play out. Understanding how a kitchen works and watching a chef plate and dress a dish continues to provide me with invaluable insights into food and wine pairing.

This may sting the pride of some, but experience has taught me that chefs are actually better at food and wine pairings than are most sommeliers. Chefs understand that a really good dish is rooted in nothing more than thoroughly understanding the relationship between basic tastes, textures and mouthfeel. I don't say this to oversimplify food, as there's an undeniable evolution in the way a dish is developed and finessed. At the restaurant level, this can get very complex. It starts by putting together simpatico ingredients, way before you arrive at balancing flavours and textures, applying the appropriate cooking technique/s and finally presenting a finished dish on the plate. A well-structured, clearly considered dish can only stand out in the endless spectrum of flavour and aroma if the basic flavour/texture relationships are in the correct balance.

Putting wine into the equation is adding another complementary element to the dish; it's the same principle. It requires equivalent consideration, not more and not less. There should be a synergy in the process of putting wine with food, and a meeting of these two elements in the middle. While you are cooking, wine choices from your collection or from a wine list should evolve logically. As you contemplate all the flavours, textures and other aspects of a particular dish, you will also be deciding what flavours and textures etc. in a wine will bring out the best in the food. Conversely, if you start from the point of view of a wine, you need to think about the impact the wine will have on the food. Of course, if you're shopping for wine for the meal, you need to ensure you already have a basic understanding of the dish.

It's when a chef first starts to build a dish – looking at key raw ingredients and deciding how to cook them – that the wine-matching magic actually starts; not when the dish is finished and maybe involves 20 different ingredients. I've learned that if you try to match wine with food at this late stage of the game, it becomes an exercise in complete confusion. Even I find it hard to know where to start. There are too many layers. What I really want you to know here, is that you can narrow your wine–food match choices right down by about 90 per cent of the entire set of possibilities, by thinking about a wine match at the very outset of cooking.

First consider the context

One of the reasons I focus on taste, texture and mouthfeel so much in this book is because these are common themes used by chefs and sommeliers alike, when compiling any food and wine offering. But another important part of this process is for the chef and sommelier to agree on a 'context' for either an entire menu of food/wine matches or for just a single dish. By context, I mean a concrete reference point, such as a cultural one, that will be shared by the dishes and the wines. A cultural reference could be French, Italian or Spanish, for example. Or, this kind of contextual starting point could involve taking an ethical approach to consumption, staying close to themes like veganism, sustainability, organics or foraging, as with the new Nordics or, what we all hope to see, which is a strong focus on vegetables and sustainable seafood, rather than defaulting to terrestrial proteins like lamb, chicken and beef.

From there, the essentials of successful food and wine pairings are actually rather simple. Building a good golf swing, for instance, is about perfecting basics such as your grip and stance, so as to form a platform for the more detailed mechanics of driving home a golf ball. If you don't have the simple basics right, your golf will suck. Bringing food and wine together in a way that is enjoyable for you, works in much the same way. You need to get the fundamentals right before you can bag the food/wine hole in one. These fundamentals are the relationships between the basic tastes, body and texture.

Body

After agreeing on some sort of context, I then find it most instructive to focus on the light-, medium- and full-bodied aspects of both the wine and food. For example, a chicken is basically a medium-bodied protein that's a good blank canvas. Of course it can take you in different directions, depending on the cooking technique and your recipe but, at the outset, think in wine-matching terms about the medium-bodied aspect of the chook and take it from there. This can ultimately lead you to anywhere from a dry riesling to a warm-climate grenache – but your basic starting point is the weight or body of the main ingredient, which should be echoed in the weight or body of the wine. Then, yes, you can look at tannins and acidity and fruit and flavour profiles and balance.

I don't think as far ahead as varieties, such as chardonnay, pinot noir or shiraz, even in a general sense. Chardonnay, as an example, is generally considered a full-bodied white, but if it comes from a particular region, or is subject to particular weather conditions or falls into the hands of a particular winemaker, it might well end up being light. All wine types can shift in this way, so you don't want to lock yourself into a rigid way of thinking about them. Wine is a natural, agricultural product, after all, subject to many variables, and not a manufactured commodity. After considering the body aspect, from here it's really all about what works for you.

Cooking techniques

The method of cooking used for a particular dish will have a dramatic impact on the ultimate wine pairing. While much of what is talked about today in regard to food and wine pairing is around flavour and aroma, very little attention is given to cooking technique.

Take a simple chicken, for example. It's a staple around the globe and the go-to ingredient for millions of us for dinner parties, barbecues and picnics. It can be poached, fried, grilled, braised and roasted, all with equal success. Each cooking technique changes the texture and taste of the chicken that opens up opportunities for wine matches – as will the ingredients you put with it. A Moroccan might make a tagine out of a chook, pairing it with warm spices, prunes, pumpkin (squash) and almonds. Give it to someone Chinese and they might poach it in soy sauce or stir-fry it in small bits with black beans, chilli, vinegar and sichuan pepper. Tuscans will likely butterfly it, marinate it in lemon juice, rosemary and garlic, then grill it under the weight of a brick. In the American south, they'll coat

WINE NOTE

I will be honest. If I am comparing myself to others who hold similar qualifications in the wine industry, I don't think I have a great nose and palate. I have never really had that innate ability that many of my peers have, where they can dissect a wine's aroma and taste with such astounding detail and clarity – it's baffling, even for someone like me. So when I started working on the restaurant floor, my education focused more on the things that came naturally to me. One of them was embracing the way I could recognise the physical nature of wine, the way it felt on my tongue and in my mouth and the way that a wine's weight and texture say as much about its origins and qualities as do descriptions of aroma and taste.

pieces of it in buttermilk and flour and deep-fry it until it's crisp and juicy. Chicken can be served on the bone or off, cooked whole, in chunks, in tiny, chopped-up pieces or minced (ground). It's got brown meat and lean white meat. It can go into a pie or curry, a wintery soup or crisp summer salad. The point I'm making is that 'chicken' is not just 'chicken'. How you cook it changes it, and this goes a long way in determining its ultimate texture and, therefore, what wine should accompany it.

STEAMING AND POACHING

These are delicate cooking techniques. They require ingredients that are light in texture, fat and flavour, such as chicken, fish, seafood, tender cuts of lean meat, fruits and vegetables. Where these two techniques get interesting, is when you add ingredients. Consider the following examples. Chicken poached in a Chinese master stock, based on soy and shaoxing wine. Fish steamed with kaffir lime leaves, ginger and lemongrass. Beef fillet (tenderloin) poached in beef stock with a bouquet garni. Seasonal fruit poached in a sugar and wine syrup with cinnamon or a vanilla bean. Scallops steamed with butter and tarragon or dill. All these elements add layers to the dish that need to be addressed from a wine perspective.

For steamed and poached dishes, look to wines that are light-bodied, which have quite high acidity, low tannins and delicate fruit flavours. Good examples are white wines like pétillant naturel sparkling wines, dry rieslings, gewürztraminer (if the food is steamed with fragrant herbs), pinot grigio, and chardonnay from the Chablis region in

France. Rosés work well here, but the paler in colour the better. Don't be afraid of reds, but look to light-bodied versions like gamay or pinot noir as a starting point.

GRILLING

Grilling is largely used on parts of an animal that are tender, have decent fat and can stand up to the merciless heat and speed of this technique. Vegetables can be grilled, too, but generally when we turn on the grill, we think of slabs of oily fish like salmon or tuna, beef steaks, pork chops, lamb cutlets and backstraps (loin), chicken thighs and sausages. It's a fundamentally simple but precise technique that highlights any flaws in an ingredient. The produce used needs to be stellar; there's no hiding behind sauces when you grill, nor is there any coming back from overcooking. Grilling makes foods juicy, full-flavoured and infused with smoke. Meats and fish are cut thick, on the whole, with a hefty weight and texture.

Avoid up-front fruitiness in wines for grilled foods and look to structure instead. Whites should lean to the medium-bodied and have good acidity and may have an element of oak. Reds will need firm tannins; they should also be medium-bodied and have decent fruit concentration. Try whites like pecorino, fiano, chenin blanc and chardonnay from slightly warmer climates. If you go for chardonnay, specify that you want a wine with oak 'texture', rather than an overt, oaky flavour and aroma. Reds are a mixed bag – dolcetto, Montepulciano, sangiovese, xinomavro, barbera and tempranillo work best.

ROASTING

Where grilling is fast, intense and a little violent, roasting is slower and more patient. Often the kinds of things you can grill are also suited to roasting – meats like lamb, beef, veal and pork. Poultry of any sort and a whole range of vegetables are good contenders, and whole fish can be roasted too. Roasting results in big, bold flavours and succulent, mouth-filling textures, commonly with an amount of fat involved. Mainly, roasted foods taste of themselves, only more intensely, although the introduction of herbs, spices, marinades, glazes, stuffings and rubs into the mix can alter flavours. Think of a sweet glazed ham, for example, or a whole chicken roasted with herb or garlic butter pushed under its skin, or a classic stuffed turkey. They all give a slightly different result.

Wine suitable for a roast usually needs to come with some muscle. White wines need to be fuller bodied and have some oak influence, higher alcohol and increased texture. Medium-bodied red wines should be used here – those that come with lots of flavour, entwined with rich, savoury wines with increased mouthfeel and soft, furry tannins. Roasting renders fats differently, breaking down tissue and tendons, releasing flavour. Roasting intensifies flavours but also adds complexity, so a wine with similar character traits is best. White blends from the Rhône Valley, malvasia, aged or wooded semillon, chardonnay and roussanne are good. Suitable reds would be nebbiolo, mencía, grenache, touriga nacional, primitivo and cool-climate shiraz (syrah).

FRYING

Deep-frying is a technique that's been reborn recently in the 'dude food' movement – where, it seems, anything and everything is dunked in a deep-fryer and seasoned with spice and salt to create the best kind of crunchily addictive snacking food imaginable. I confess that I love it. For the longest time, deep-frying was such a dirty word, connected as it was with our collective horror of fats and fear of an unhealthy diet.

But frying isn't about eating food dripping with copious oil. When done right, its effects can be subtle, refined and respectful of produce. Fried at the correct temperature, foods shouldn't absorb too much of the oil, but simply use it as the cooking medium. Think of Japanese tempura, for example, which is ridiculously light and delicate. Anything from tender zucchini (courgette) blossoms to seafood, to chunks of pork or chicken or cheese can be deep-fried; they need to be coated to protect their surface and when that coating is thick, like a batter, food essentially steams inside.

A category of wines that works well with fried food is skin-contact white wines (see page 139). The salty, spicy, umami notes in fried food latches onto the fresh acidity and savoury characters in skin-contact white wine. It has the same effect as beer – it cools spice, cuts fat and softens salt, making it dangerously more-ish. When you ask for skin-contact wines, don't ask for the grape or region, just ask for a 'skin-contact white', but emphasise you want it 'fresh'. This should ensure the sommelier or retailer gets you a wine that's not too whacky and still suits the food.

WINE NOTE

I always emphasise weight and texture when bringing food and wine together. I match food and wine in terms of their compatible structure, not taste and aroma. There are literally millions of compounds to detect in wine and, sometimes, the detecting of them can be individual. YOU might pick up things that I don't – if you smell geraniums and spam in a wine and I get daffodils and smoked salmon, all power to you. This is about giving you confidence so you don't feel like a dick when talking to a wine professional, whether at the wine shop, online or at a restaurant.

Pan-frying is a slightly different technique, suited to thin fillets or cutlets of fish, vegetables or meat. These may be lightly crumbed, floured or otherwise coated in a protective element – but not necessarily. So, the exteriors of fried foods span the entire range of textural possibilities, from soft, light and thin to thick, rich and crunchy.

When pairing wine with food that has been cooked with fat, the number one thing you need is acid. Acidity cleans the palate; it strips the fatty stuff out of your tastebuds and refreshes your mouth. The more fat, the more acid you need, but never at the expense of the balance between texture and taste. Interestingly, oak can also play a role here.

Generally with frying, the darker the exterior becomes, the more oak you need in your white wine. So if you are only lightly frying (say, fish in a pan), then a light- to medium-bodied dry white with little or no oak might suit. But if you deep-fry, or get a good dark crust on the food, then an oaked wine, like a chardonnay, works better. Oak flavours have a great relationship with the rich, toasty flavours of frying.

When pairing wine with food that has been cooked with fat, the number one thing you need is acid.

BRAISING AND STEWING

Slow cooking in liquid is a long process where consistent and gentle heat is applied over an extended period of time. This type of cooking breaks down and tenderises cuts of meat that would otherwise be tough and dry. Hardworking cuts like shoulder, brisket and shanks, full of hard connective tissues, are perfect candidates for braising and stewing. Those tissues break down over time in the pot, becoming unctuous and lip-smackingly tender, while cooking liquids take on a deep, meaty and memorable richness. Stewing and braising tends to speak more to cooler months when dishes need to be hearty, and flavours robust and warming. Matching wines to braises and stews really depends on the depth, richness and concentration of flavour in the finished dish.

Medium- to full bodied wines are the best bet. You need soft, not aggressive, tannins. Look for a balanced fruit character that matches the level of tannin; a good level of sweetness and alcohol helps as well. Aged wine works well with these sorts of dishes, especially fuller bodied, high-tannin reds whose texture and concentrations of flavour match the intensity of the food; those tannins should have softened over time, though. It really comes down to the ingredients here, especially the protein you are using. Whites, semillon and sauvignon blanc blends from Bordeaux, grüner veltliner, pinot gris, viognier and skin-contact whites work with white proteins. Red proteins like beef or lamb need mourvèdre, cabernet sauvignon, grenache, nero d'Avola, cabernet franc and shiraz.

Putting it all together: making a great match

Now, let's look at some real-world scenarios to illustrate what I mean by all the information discussed above and in the previous chapter. First, I'll take a classic pairing – oysters and dry riesling – and try to figure out why this combo works and what the two elements, oysters and riesling, have in common that make them so perfect for each other. (And if you don't like oysters, substitute salmon for this exercise.)

Oysters are light-bodied, salty, delicate and creamy.
Riesling is light-bodied, acidic and crisp.

Is this a light-bodied match? Yes. For the rest, the acid in the wine complements the salt in the oysters, and creamy food textures are complemented by crisp ones in wine. There's a harmony here that's perfect – and notice we're not using fancy wine words to describe any flavours or aromas.

Next, let's tread another well-worn path, this time putting prosciutto with pinot noir.

Prosciutto is light-bodied and fatty.
Pinot noir is light-bodied and acidic.

Is this a light-bodied match? Yes. And the acid in the wine works to cut the fat in the food; so, it's an ideal combination.

In both of these examples, the weight and texture of the wine and of the food are the first gateways you need to pass through. I can't say this enough: don't stress about what the taste of the prosciutto is, or what the aroma of the pinot noir is. Unless you get that all-important weight and texture match right in the first instance, you won't be left with anything that allows you to appreciate the flavours of the wine or the food!

SIZE AND FIT

Now, let's look at the same piece of produce used across several dishes and cooked differently in each dish. Here we're using beef. And this is interesting as there's a thing called the 'Glass Slipper' effect at work here, where the 'size' and 'fit' of a key ingredient affect mouthfeel, and thus the body and texture in a wine, influencing the choice of wine to match.

There's a huge difference between a slice of beef carpaccio (incredibly thin, delicate and raw) and a grilled piece of eye fillet (thick, chewy, juicy and a little smoky), even though they are essentially the exact same ingredient. The carpaccio is light-bodied, the steak is full-bodied. In each instance, they will require a totally different wine.

If we start looking at each dish listed below and, by measuring the weight, texture, intensity of flavour and the cooking technique employed in each, we can start to include a wider selection of wines in our tasting toolkit. Notice how the glass slipper effect comes into play. These examples will give you some idea of the approach I take when working on the floor with diners, suggesting wine matches for their meal. It's also the same approach I use when consulting with a chef as to what should go on the wine list to complement a certain dish or dishes.

LIGHT-BODIED RED WINE MATCH

Beef tartare is delicate, raw, fatty, spicy and tender.

Notice the way I've broken this dish down into a list of simple words that sum up its very essence. I've not discussed in detail how the dish contains capers, raw onion, Tabasco, egg yolk, cornichons, mustard, chopped parsley and so on. Beef tartare is really quite a complex dish in terms of its ingredients, but if you start thinking about a potential wine match with those things uppermost, you'll become too tangled up in all the specific elements and flavours and get lost. It becomes way too hard.

What wine people like me do is break a complex dish like this down into the sorts of words I've used here – and only a few of them. We then use those words in a taste-centric way by literally saying, 'OK, what wine will go with foods that are described using these words?'

For a wine to work with beef tartare, I can see that I need something light-bodied, with a small measure of tannin to work with the delicate and raw nature of the protein. Plus, there should be some subtle fruit intensity to work with the warm spice hit (usually from Tabasco sauce). I will need low-range tannins and high-range acidity, with a sweet but delicate fruit character to cope with the spice and heat. Low levels of oak and alcohol are required, too, as oak and alcohol could easily overwhelm the delicate, but intense, nature of the food. I want to have the wine sitting just beneath the food in terms of its concentration of weight and taste, and this is important. Wine should always sit below food in this way, otherwise it risks overwhelming the dish.

> I want to have the wine sitting just beneath the food in terms of its concentration of weight and taste ...

MEDIUM-BODIED RED WINE MATCH

Wagyu bresaola is cured, fatty, smoky, rich and thinly sliced.

Here's where you can start to have a bit of fun. Bresaola requires a medium-bodied wine and these represent wines with plenty of flavour and freshness. They have structure but in a firm, engaging way. The fat in the food is the link here; you need the right pitch of acidity to cut through it, and a good concentration of flavour to match the intensity and saltiness that come from curing and ageing the meat. Finally, tannins should be soft and savoury. Thinly sliced aged meat would be overwhelmed by the big chunky tannins that you find in a full-bodied red wine.

FULL-BODIED RED WINE MATCH

Wagyu beef eye fillet is rich, fatty, full-flavoured, a big piece of protein and smoky.

I'd want a wine here with more 'volume', more texture and more weight, to match that thicker cut and bigger portion of protein. I need more tannin and richer fruit flavours, plus there should be a good level of acidity to cut the fat. Importantly, I don't want a wine that competes with the beef. Remember, you want a wine that sits just beneath the dish in terms of concentration of taste and texture.

Note, I'm deliberately NOT giving you actual wine names here, or even specific varieties. I want you to start thinking about wines for yourself, and begin having confidence in your own abilities to work good matches out. Some wine writers – and a lot of populist wine literature – might give you a prescription – a this-goes-with-that kind of a list. However, I'm trying to take you away from that approach.

Remember, there's no such thing as perfection. Every time you discuss a food and wine pairing, everything is academic until you get both in your mouth. For sure, there are certain combinations that simply don't work, due to undeniable conflict in basic taste or texture. Red wines with lots of tannins will never be compatible with a freshly shucked oyster for instance. What we are discussing here are boundaries and not rules. The boundaries exist so we know there are some things that are and are not OK in food and wine pairing. What takes place within those boundaries is all about personal taste and experimentation. When we talk about basic taste, weight and texture, we are simply drawing the boundary lines so that we can start. From there, the wine you choose comes down to personal taste. Don't try to be perfect; perfection doesn't exist in wine decision making. However, consider the following basics.

Flexibility in wine

For a great many years, ideas around wine quality centred around softness of texture, sweetness of flavour and a high alcohol by volume (ABV). Wines fought to stand out in wine shows, media tastings and in the mass retail market, based on these elements. At the lower priced end of the market, wineries would devote their energies to creating products full of sweetness and alcohol as they tried to out-muscle each other in this domain.

As wine became more 'internationalised' in the 1980s and 1990s (that is, more wines from different markets became more widely available across different markets), it also became 'industrialised' to cope with the increased demand from new and emerging markets. Because of a relentless quest to achieve lower prices and broad appeal, wines aiming for the same type of consumer all started to look pretty much the same. The same sweetness and alcohol infused into these wines, to broaden their appeal, sacrificed structural characteristics such as acidity and tannin. These days we're seeing acidity and tannin as highly desirable in wine, particularly where food is concerned.

Real progress in recent years has been made by winemakers who have lowered the levels of sweetness, oak and alcohol in their wines. These characteristics, when in high concentration, overwhelm your sense of taste. Food requires wine to 'give' a bit on the palate, and the changing nature of wine is shifting towards increased acidity and lighter, softer, more savoury tannins. These wines have become not only more drinkable but also easier to partner with food. These wines are more responsive to other tastes and textures and have what I call 'flexibility' – or just 'flex'.

In simple terms, flex is the measurement of a wine's ability to react to food. While flex is not exclusive to any one grape variety or wine style, there is no doubt some types of wine exhibit more flex than others. More and more wines are showing good flex; they're savoury and fresh, giving them the malleability that makes their relationship with food so exciting and rewarding.

This idea of flex is central to my work and my relationship with food. I like to imagine a scale of flex like a car tachometer, which is a device that measures revolutions per minute, or 'RPMs', of a car's engine, going up in increments of 1 to 10, with 10 being the highest on the scale and the ideal place being at 5. A 10-flex wine will be the same as over-revving your engine. It will be a really thick specimen that won't give an inch when paired with food. A 1-flex wine

is like under-revving the engine. It will be watery, thin wine that will be overwhelmed by food. A 5-flex is the middle ground, just like an engine 'in gear', where the balance between fruit, acidity and tannin is in harmony – for me, a nebbiolo is probably the greatest example of a wine with a number 5 flex. Flex, or lack of it, can be corrected with food and that's why it's such an important, and exciting concept to understand.

Think of most wines as having a slight imbalance between elements of fruit, tannin and acidity. Very few are actually perfect in this regard, for a whole variety of reasons. Now think of food as holding the key to smoothing out those imperfections and rounding out the wine. Here's an example to illustrate what I mean.

I remember being in Greece and drinking a xinomavro – a native red that's notorious for its high acidity and tannins that really rip into your gums. I wasn't particularly enjoying it; it tasted completely out of whack to me. But then I drank it with a hefty serve of roast lamb, and the story around that wine was a completely different one. The sweetness and fattiness of the lamb subdued the tannins and acid in the wine and, suddenly, I was in love with xinomavro. The elements in the food 'corrected' the perceived lack of harmony in the wine – without food, the wine didn't make much sense. That's flex at work. It's a wine's ability to 'move' or 'bend' with food in order to become more harmonious. Happily, more and more red wines today are being made with a focus on acidity and tannin and are not fruit-sweetened and alcoholic. The result? They're more food-friendly and drinkable, with greater degrees of flex.

Where food goes, wine follows

I'm hoping you're starting to see how intertwined the relationship is between chefs, sommeliers, wine, food and what you ultimately end up cooking and drinking at home. Sommeliers have become communicators, as well as procurers and educators. They reflect the nature of the modern dining experience, where food and wine are now, more than ever, constituting a single conversation rather than two separate ones. Understanding these concepts leads, I think, to a better understanding of wine and food and what our relationship should be with them. Basically, you could say that where food goes, wine follows, which can be seen in emerging trends in both food and wine, like a 'call and response' effect.

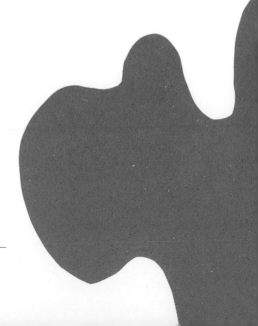

NEW FOOD,
NEW WINE

The food and wine choices you're making at home right now are influenced by what's currently happening in restaurant culture. The restaurants we dine in, or even just read about, reflect evolving trends in food across the spectrum and these trickle down to inform the way we think about food generally. Whether it's the rise of 'haute' fast food, where simple diners turn out exemplary southern fried chicken, gourmet burgers or American barbecue; or the pointier end of things where complex, vegetable-based degustation menus are a 'thing', the professional hospitality scene has an impact on the way we consider, cook and serve food. Even if we're not dining at their restaurants, many of the chefs we admire are now celebrities in their own right and we are probably buying their cookbooks, following them on social media or reading about them in our favourite food magazines. At any rate, we look to them both for inspiration and guidance and we absorb their influence, as it gradually pervades the general food culture.

It's a subtle effect. But, as a result of all these threads of influence, home cooks are – in my opinion – becoming ever more adventurous. They're buying ingredients with a better-developed eye to provenance, seasonality and quality than they previously did. Conversely, when they do eat at those leading restaurants, they're also more intrepid, and willing to open themselves up to new flavours, textures and combinations.

So, how is this relevant to wine? Well, in the same way that good restaurant chefs are informing our food choices and cooking styles, so too are good sommeliers influencing what wines we drink, and what we drink them with. This influence might not be so overt as that of the chefs – because sommeliers don't get the same star-status press as those guys and gals do, but the direction that food travels in inevitably takes wine along for the ride, too. Specific styles of food demand specific types of wines to match with them and, if there's an overall shift in the way we are dining, it stands to reason there's a corresponding shift in the types of wines being produced, to complement those changes.

The evolving food scene

To best illustrate this idea that the changes in the food scene (and therefore the changing food–wine relationship that results from this) influence how we eat, I'd point to some significant recent shifts. I'd highlight, for example, Scandinavian restaurants like Fäviken in Sweden, and Noma in Denmark, both at the forefront of the foraging, garden-centric, locavore movement, which is a defining hallmark of modern Nordic cuisine. Such establishments have spiked global interest with their unconventional cooking techniques, such as smoking, salting and fermentation – maybe not unusual in themselves, but are applied by these guys in unexpected ways.

These concepts filter through the food chain, not just to high-end restaurants but all the way down to casual cafes, cookbooks and, ultimately, down to you, the home cook and food enthusiast. You see it in the cookbooks you buy that extol preserving, fermenting and foraging. Along the way, new trends pose challenges for the sommelier (and wine drinker), making them think outside the box when attempting to come up with relevant pairings for dishes with combinations of textures and flavours never seen before.

The new generation of chefs is also taking a more 'primal' approach to produce, by buying top-quality ingredients and using every part they possibly can. This trend is not only bound up in ethics and sustainability but also in flavour and texture. All parts of a beast or plant are being utilised. Broccoli stalks. Bone marrow. Carrot greens. Pig's ears and tails. Blood. Parsnip peels. Fennel fronds. While the anti-waste aspect of this trend has thrown up the tongue-in-cheek term 'compost cookery', I believe this 'root to shoot', 'nose to tail' movement reflects a new respect for ingredients that's deeper than chefs have ever had before. Obviously, cost-conscious chefs don't want anything to end up in the bin, but this movement is driven as much by social conscience as it is by thrift.

How does the sommelier respond to not just these new flavours, textures and combinations, but also these new attitudes and awareness towards eating and food?

To answer that question, in part at least, I'd highlight yet another, more general trend in food that's been steadily gaining pace, which is having an enormous impact on the types of wines we drink. This is the preference for healthier eating, which, niftily, runs in harmonious tandem with the other trends I've just mentioned. More and more of us want a lower refined-sugar consumption, we want to eat more fruit and vegetables, to consume healthier types of fats and cut back on refined grains and other carbs. The kinds of wines that go with this 'cleaner' style of eating aren't the sweetly fruited, high-alcohol wines that were once so popular. Younger, fresher, drier wines with lower alcohol content answer the needs of newer, healthier ways of eating and, increasingly, over the years, these are the sorts of food-friendly wines I am working with.

Response from the wine industry

At the grassroots level, the wine industry has responded to the evolution of our palate and our dining preferences by producing types of wines that are in tune with emerging food styles (see page 135.) There are clear dining parallels with these values-based wine choices and they work like this: the sommelier brings these newer wines to the attention of diners who are in search of appropriate pairings – with what chefs are now bringing to the table – which is in line with prevailing food trends. For example, there's even a vegan movement in wine, where non-animal derived fining agents, such as fine clay, are being used to filter wine in place of the more traditional ones like egg white and blood.

Younger, fresher, drier wines with lower alcohol content answer the needs of newer, healthier ways of eating ...

Even though winemakers are now expressing themselves in whole new types of winemaking ways, and are toying with some weird and wonderful grape varieties, these are still rooted, as are all wines, in the fundamentals of taste, texture and mouthfeel (see page 39). Whether you're the one making the wine or the one drinking it, you need to understand these basics before you can take them and run with them in either scenario.

This new generation of winemakers feel they don't have to adhere to the traditional interpretation of a variety or region. This generational shift going on in wineries and vineyards means change. This change could be in the form of new grape varieties, a new region and new way of blending, or even a change in the way a wine is made. Change can also be taking established subject matter, like chardonnay, and 'twisting' it.

Australian chardonnay has had quite the reputation: big, bold, busty wines packed with oak and alcohol; wines that had their moment in history and for many wine drinkers still remain relevant today. However, the growth of cool-climate viticulture in Australia has exploded due to the demand for lighter, fresher wines for newer drinkers. New and established winemakers are now responding to this through touchpoints like chardonnay, because it makes discovering new wines a comfortable experience. Chardonnay can be rich and full, but it can also be refreshing and crisp. It can be puffed up with oak or have none at all. It can be matured in oak, steel or clay pots.

All the shifts and trends in winemaking and viticulture can be seen through grape varieties and regions that are both new and well known. However, what doesn't alter is the winemakers' and grape growers' drive to evolve. They are creating wines that are clearly holding themselves accountable to their origins but are almost unrecognisable in their texture and mouthfeel. They see wine not just in colour, flavour and aroma but in texture and shape; thereby creating wines that are long, lean and straight, through to rich and round, but all anchored in a balance between wine's most fundamental components: acidity, tannin, concentration of flavour, alcohol and, in some cases, oak.

This approach to grape growing and winemaking yields a wine that is immediately drinkable and enjoyable with food.

New wines – and old

Every generation has its Zeitgeist wine. For my parents' generation, it was richly proportioned, oak-driven white wines made from chardonnay, and full-flavoured, high-alcohol, broad-shouldered red wines made from shiraz and cabernet. As I entered the wine industry, I saw it embrace aromatic white wines made from sauvignon blanc and riesling, and lighter, more restrained red wines made from pinot noir. Excitingly, there are tons of new ways wines are being made. Comparing the number of grape varieties and different wine styles of the past to the wine industry of today is like comparing the amount of songs on a vinyl record to the catalogue of music available on iTunes. There is no doubt that this explosion in diversity comes down to a new generation of wine drinkers who are more curious, better educated and more discerning about value than ever before.

Interestingly, some winemakers are reaching back into the past to revive old techniques. These techniques not only introduce new and exciting textures and tastes, but also open up possibilities for food compatibility. Some of the techniques that are influencing the wines you are drinking today include the following.

Interestingly, some winemakers are reaching back into the past to revive old techniques. These techniques not only introduce new and exciting textures and tastes, but also open up possibilities for food compatibility.

PÉTILLANT NATUREL

'Pét nat' is nothing new. In fact, it's probably one of the oldest methods of making wine known to humankind. Another name for this technique of winemaking is 'méthode ancestrale', and it's used to describe a wine that's bottled before primary fermentation is completed, without adding any secondary yeasts or sugars. This isn't to be confused with 'méthode champenoise', used to make Champagne, where the finished wine goes through a secondary fermentation in the bottle, giving it bubble, plus more alcohol and complexity from contact with the yeast left over after fermentation is finished, called lees.

Essentially, the pét nat method halts the fermentation, retaining bubbles but reducing alcohol and creating a unique texture. Wines made this way are super affordable and they rank high on the drinkability scale, due to their more 'textural' nature. They're not 'pretty' wines, but they're not meant to be. Rather, pét nats are often unfiltered and cloudy, with a wide range of bubble sizes due to the use of more localised and natural yeasts in their production. They're rustic and simple, with a freshness and full, grapy flavours and they represent exceptional value on a wine list.

Today's wine drinkers see sparkling wine as a less serious wine – more casual, celebratory and fun. The retail versions of this type of wine are prosecco and moscato, while the restaurant version is pét nat. Prosecco and moscato are fruity, frothy wines and, in the case of moscato, can often be quite perfumed and sweet. Pét nats are more wine-like and carry more of the variety and region's signature taste, texture, flavour and aroma.

OXIDISED WINES

A real interest in oxidised wines has emerged over the last decade and these have helped reset popular ideas around taste and flavour. By exposing a wine in a slow, controlled way to oxygen (during the winemaking and maturation process), you not only alter the colour of the wine but also the aroma and taste. In the high-volume, brand-driven wine arena, a wine's quality has traditionally been judged on the pristine quality of its fruit and attractive aromas. Oxidised wine was always seen as 'faulty'. But from a basic taste perspective, these wines are riddled with that elusive fifth taste called umami (see page 94), which in a wine translates to an earthy, savoury and mouthwatering quality. This umami quality is why oxidised wines found such a willing home in wine bars and restaurants, long before the rest of the wine market cottoned onto them. They're just so good with food!

At a molecular level, contact with oxygen causes substances to change or degrade. This includes wine. A badly oxidised wine is one that's suffered from too much oxygen exposure and it loses all brightness of colour and flavour – it may even turn brownish. I remember the first time I saw that famous, iron-rich, red soil of South Australia's Coonawarra wine region. The reddening or rusting of the soil was the effect of oxygen. Judicious, controlled oxygen exposure in the winemaking process is a way to deliberately move a wine away from being fruity to being more savoury, earthy and complex.

Contact with air is something that producers of commercial white wines avoid as it can dull aromatics and flavours in a category where simplicity and consistency are largely the goal. Why does this matter? For me, the answer is in the way that white wines with oxidative character

THE JURA

The Jura is a tiny French wine region just inside the Swiss border, and the wines from there are some of the most delicious and mouthwatering in the world. It shouldn't come as a surprise then to learn that most of them – from the lighter bodied and refreshing ones to the deeply coloured, richly textured, aged 'vin jaune' – are made with varying levels of controlled oxidation.

respond to food. Imagine you have two wines made from the same grape variety. Wine A has been exposed to oxygen during winemaking, while Wine B has been protected from it. The pretty, fruity Wine B will require a lighter touch with food so as not to be overwhelmed by it. Wine A, with its oxidative character, will demand more complexity in a food match. It will really rise to the occasion when you throw more robustly flavoured food into the mix.

I talk a lot about oxidation in this book as it's such an important thread currently running through wine. At one point, even I was slightly clueless about the importance of it and the way oxidation could open wine up to food in an incredible way.

Some years back I was in Slovenia, judging at a wine show. There were plenty of wines from that part of the Adriatic to taste and, to my mind, they were pretty ghastly – oxidised like all get-out and, to me, absolutely riven with faults. I marked them low – very low – until the chief judge hauled me aside and asked me to scale up my marks. 'But

these wines are oxidised!' I spluttered. 'They're faulty'.
He just looked at me and said, 'That's how we make our
wines around here. It's how they're meant to taste.' Later
that night, I was taken on a cruise on the Adriatic, and all
the local food came out. Mainly it was barbecued seafood
caught from the ocean that day. There was lamb, grilled
local vegetables and boat-loads of freshly baked bread.
It was simple fare but delicious, with chewy, salty, charred,
sweet, gutsy flavours and textures. The wines that went
with this feast were also wonderful, so supple and more-ish
and I couldn't get enough of them. When I commented on
the wines, I found out they were exactly the ones I'd made
such a song and dance about at the wine show that day. It
was as though I was drinking something entirely different.
That was the effect of food on what I'd dismissed as harsh,
unpleasant, oxidised wines. This was such a lesson for me
in all kinds of things. I now appreciated there was a different
approach to the pretty, perfect 'show' wines I'd been used
to tasting and that, with the right kind of food, wines made
with controlled oxidation could really soar. It made me view
oxidation in an entirely different light.

SKIN CONTACT

The idea of 'soaking' juice and skin together to impart
colour to wine is one of the world's oldest winemaking
techniques. Until recently, though, this was a process
almost exclusively used for making red wine. During the red
winemaking process, this mixture of soaked flesh and skin
is pressed, after a time, to extract tannins. However, where
'skin contact' is really becoming relevant for modern wine

GEORGIAN SKIN-CONTACT WINES

Georgia is a country nestled between the coastline of the Black Sea and its former landlord, Russia. Making wine, and drinking it in weapons-grade amounts, is in the Georgians' DNA, and they have been making and drinking wine for over 8000 years. Much of their wine is made with skin contact and is where they get their well-known orange or amber hue. Much of Eastern Europe has a wine culture with a history and longevity that dwarfs that of France and Italy. Watch to see more wines from this part of the world on wine lists everywhere – just make sure you decant them!

drinkers is actually in white wine. The skins of white grapes not only give additional colour to white wine but also introduce tannins – although not in the same concentration as you'll find in red wines. As well as a tannic hit, that skin contact also adds a textural and savoury aspect to white wines that traditionally we haven't seen before.

Skin contact is what's behind the 'orange' wines that are proliferating currently; these wines are getting their name from the slightly orange hue they receive from skin maceration. As someone who is trying to sell you the idea that food and wine are a single conversation, I will openly say I love the idea of skin contact. It gives white wines more body and texture but at the same time makes them more flexible and responsive to food. White wines with skin contact will have a slightly deeper 'blush' colour than regular whites and feel drier in your mouth, due to the presence of low-level tannins. Note that these sorts of whites require decanting and should be served with food.

NATURAL WINE

The term 'natural wine' has no real legal definition. It's more an idea and a philosophical approach to winemaking, so it's not something that you'll necessarily see on a wine label. It's an ethos that says the earth and the vine deserve respect, and is a recognition that the winemaker has only a temporary assignment, where the earth is concerned. 'Natural' winemaking is as much about what you *don't* do to a wine as what you *do* do to it. It's a more bespoke approach, rather than one that tries to make wines that appeal to a broad commercial base. (A wine being 'natural' doesn't reduce your chance of a hangover, either, in case you were wondering!)

What we mean by natural wine is wine as it was originally made over 8000 years ago – before chemicals and additives and well before the excessive manipulation of wine through winemaking became popular. Intervention in the making or maturation of a wine allows a winemaker to achieve a critical balance between vineyard, variety and winemaker in the wine. A natural wine will be less polished; it may even have a few rough edges and a greater amount of texture than what you are used to. It's bound to have more complexity coming from a greater influence of oxygen and skins. It may even have some characteristics that could be potentially dismissed as faults. However, it's important not to label these as such.

I look at natural wines this way, via a food analogy. There was a time when we only celebrated luxury cuts of an animal, such as the eye fillet (tenderloin) of beef, the loin of pork, the backstrap (fillet) of lamb, the breast of a chicken. Secondary meats like cheeks, tails, offal (variety meats) and tough braising cuts were eschewed – especially when you dined out. But now every bit of an animal or bird is championed. Natural wines are part of this same mentality – they're a bit primal-tasting and different from what we're used to, and maybe even inelegant at times. But they deserve acceptance for their unique characteristics and the thought that goes into making them. The texture, smells and tastes we turn our nose up at today could well become the accepted character of the everyday wine we drink in the very near future.

'WHOLE BUNCH'

This is an even more 'primal' approach to winemaking, especially when applied to light- and medium-bodied red wines. Making wines this way boosts texture and mouthfeel, without adding elements like overt flavours of oak. Whole bunch winemaking is where winemakers include the entire grape bunch, including stalks, in the winemaking and don't filter out these parts until the grape juice is ready for fermentation to become wine. Conventional winemaking wisdom has it that only the grape variety holds the key to the right sort of refined flavour a wine should have. But lately, growers and winemakers are looking beyond the ultimate ripe grape berry and to the entire grape bunch as a source of not just aroma and taste, but texture and mouthfeel, too.

Again, this has clear parallels to what's happening in food, where there's a real reluctance to waste anything. In previous decades, menus tended to showcase only the pristine, aesthetically pleasing, perfectly portioned versions of meat, seafood, poultry and produce. There was, to my mind, an air of excess to this.

The new tradition being written by contemporary chefs is to celebrate produce in its entirety, seeing bones, tendons, skin, organs and fats as important sources of texture and flavour. Not only is this approach more sustainable and respectful, it's also one that unlocks incredible amounts of texture and flavour. Think of a beautifully made meat-based stock and you'll know instantly what I mean. Skin, bones, connective tissue and bits of meat – it all goes into the pot with water and, over the course of a few hours, is rendered into something incredible. There's real texture from collagen and elastin, and lip-smacking flavour from bones, marrow, fat and meat. So it is with whole bunch wines, where extra tannins are released from the stalks and skins. These tannins are softer, more savoury and more malleable. They are not the big, blocky, sweet and cumbersome tannins from heavy-handed new oak or high extraction. (Extraction is the process of pressing the mix of skin, seed and/or stalks. This is a red wine-making technique, as white grapes have their juice and skins separated prior to the wine going through fermentation.) This process will extract more tannins that could overpower and dominate a dish. When used in judicious measure, solids like skins, stalks and seeds can add layers of tannin that unwind spectacularly with food.

NEW WHITE WINES

ASSYRTIKO Super dry, salty and fresh with texture and a mouthwatering acidity – the new Petit Chablis. Try this if you like chardonnay from Chablis, France.

UGNI BLANC A racy, clean, linear white, which can be quite neutral but also somewhat fruity when produced in warmer climates. Try this if you like semillon.

GRECO DI TUFO Aromatic, crisp and clean – a great aperitif white wine when you want buckets of acidity to spark your appetite. Try this if you like pinot grigio.

FIANO A medium-bodied, fruity, nice alternative white with a spicy, savoury-edged palate. Try this if you like pinot gris.

FURMINT A medium-bodied, soft, rich, but ultimately elegant wine. It can have higher alcohol, which can add to the wine's body and mouthfeel.

CHENIN BLANC Medium-bodied, supple, textural, elegant and super fresh – this can age for decades if stored well. Try this if you like sauvignon blanc.

ROUSSANNE Medium- to full-bodied, soft, rich and ultimately elegant wine that can have higher alcohol, giving it extra body and mouthfeel. Try this if you like chardonnay.

NEW RED WINES

GRENACHE Medium- to full-bodied and usually blended with shiraz and mourvèdre; grenache is about to have its real moment as a single variety. Think of it as warm-climate pinot noir; where it's grown is more important than how it's made.

AGLIANICO A full-bodied, sturdy wine known for its earthy flavours, mouth-filling tannins and savoury-edged palate. Try this if you like cabernet sauvignon.

CABERNET FRANC Medium-bodied, this is the cabernet you want when you don't want a cabernet. A great alternative to cabernet sauvignon, with its inky colour and wads of fruit flavour wrapped in softer, more pliable tannins. It tends to be well priced. Try this if you like cabernet merlot blends.

NEBBIOLO Light- to medium-bodied, this is like pinot noir but with the volume turned up a few notches. Super savoury with high tannins and high acidity, this is wine with more 'flex' than most. Try this if you like pinot noir.

NERO D'AVOLA Full-bodied, rich, soft and grippy, this wine is full of dark fruits, rich tannin and powerful flavours. It's purpose-built for those who like the broad-shouldered wines made from shiraz or zinfandel.

SAGRANTINO Medium- to full-bodied, rippling with high acidity and high tannins. It's a good alternative if you like cabernet sauvignon.

SAPERAVI Medium-bodied and dry with high acidity levels and firm, savoury tannins. It can taste a little wild and needs to be served with fatty, protein-based foods.

TOURIGA NACIONAL A full-bodied red from a grape usually reserved for port production. Expect thickly textured wines that are perforated with firm, chalky tannins. Another red for lovers of full-throttle wines. Try this if you like shiraz.

XINOMAVRO Medium- to full-bodied, this is a wine packed with grippy, savoury tannins and bristling with a spiky, crackling acidity with gobs of flavour and a dense, chewy texture. Try this if you like nebbiolo with the volume turned up.

NEW WINES

GRAPE EXPECTATIONS – NEW FRUIT

Despite lingering debate in some quarters around the causes, you can't argue that our climate is definitely changing. Extreme weather is becoming more commonplace and this affects the delicate balance within the ecosystems that are vineyards. The fact that our climate is changing means our grape diet will also ultimately have to change, too. Increasing average temperatures mean we are going to require more heat-tolerant, drought-resistant grape varieties than some of those we currently rely on. Grapes will also need to be able to thrive on less water, too. It is safe to imagine that the retail wine shelf or wine list you look at today will have a very different appearance in the future.

As to what these wines will be made from or taste like, it's probable they are already on good wine lists, even though they're not yet mainstream. This is how wine should exist in the wine bar or restaurant – quality driven and offering a glimpse into a much bigger world that is turbo-charged by awareness, education and curiosity, and a wine industry making more and more wines built around regionalism, diversity and gastronomy.

See the chart on pages 144–5 for a list of some of the new varieties that are popping up on wine lists. They reflect the growing diversity in wine. They're listed in increasing intensity of mouthfeel and texture.

Looking to the future

Growing up and working in the restaurant industry over the last 25 years, I have seen the dramatic shifts in what we eat and drink first hand. The popularity of new varietals and wine styles begins in restaurant and wine bars. This is where the credibility of new ideas and real evolution is sown.

In the future more countries will enter the global wine market, more new varieties will appear and more regions will come online. More information will be available and more opinions will be offered. Essentially, there will just be more of everything.

If I am looking to the future in restaurants, then wine is entering a real golden age. In a dining scenario, diversity is something to be celebrated. I think the big wine lists will go the way of the dinosaurs. Shorter lists, which are more succinct, will appear to combat the inevitable rising operating costs. Bio-dynamics and organics will increase in relevance, as will the importance of regionalism in wine.

After so many years of working with chefs, winemakers, growers, producers and customers, I still believe that if you want to see the future in wine, look at how we are eating today. If history teaches us anything, it's that where our stomach goes our palate will follow.

THE RESTAURANT EXPERIENCE

All that work put in by the people behind the wine ... it all comes down to this moment in time, when the wine is delivered to you and poured into a glass.

When a bottle of wine is opened in a restaurant, it's a seminal moment. All that work put in by the people behind the wine – the grape grower, winemaker, salesman, marketers and distributors – it all comes down to this moment in time, when the wine is delivered to you and poured into a glass.

Wine in a restaurant becomes a mosaic of taste, texture, flavour and aroma – a snapshot of all that the winemaker sought to achieve. And a good wine list can be a window into a much bigger wine world than perhaps you are familiar with; it can push you into new corners of that world. Without someone to help you navigate this, even the most experienced drinker can become lost.

One of the great evolutions that I have seen in the wine industry over the last 20 years is the increasing effectiveness of wine professionals in hospitality as advocates for wine. They tell the stories around wine as powerfully as they communicate ideas around texture, taste, flavour and aroma. Wine service staff are actually the last point of contact between the winemaker and the wine drinker and, as such, they play a really important role in representing a particular wine. Increasingly, the person to whom this responsibility falls is the sommelier. The sommelier is your guide, not a teacher. Helping a guest make an informed choice from a wine list is the sommelier's real goal.

The restaurant wine experience

During my career I've noted how communication around wine can be way more effective than even structured wine education. This takes people away from preconceived expectations and into the realm of discovering their own taste. Representing wine in a restaurant is essentially a sales and marketing role – I get that. And I know many people are a tad cynical about being up-sold or ripped off, or approached at their table with the sale in mind, not the purpose of engagement or communication. But I still love how pumped people become when I actually engage with them about wine. I love it when regular customers in a restaurant look to me to suggest something new, or special, or daring, because we've built up trust over time and they know I'll bring something to the table that speaks to their taste and will make their night even better. My job is to add to the total sum of their restaurant visit by creating an experience around wine that's comfortable, informative and enjoyable. Why am I saying all of this? Because I think that understanding what the restaurant experience has to offer, helps broaden and shape your understanding of wine – because wine is so integral to it.

The wine experience in a restaurant is unique. You won't see the same wines on a wine list that you'll see in popular wine stores. That's because restaurant staff build direct relationships with distributors, wholesalers and winemakers, who supply them with limited releases and other special bits and pieces that the general public can't easily get their hands on. In restaurants at the moment, there's a real call-to-arms to support 'small' winemaking practices, and the wines coming out of this genre aren't the ones that tend to populate mainstream wine shelves. 'Small' winemaking techniques aren't to do with the physical size of a winery,

> **I love it when regular customers in a restaurant look to me to suggest something new, or special, or daring, because we've built up trust over time and they know I'll bring something to the table that speaks to their taste and will make their night even better.**

IT'S NOT JUST ABOUT THE WINE

Along with the wine, of course the food and the restaurant service are pretty important, too. For a restaurant to do well, all of these elements have to be excellent. And there is so much good food to be found today. Young, dynamic chefs are pushing boundaries and sending a powerful message to diners that food matters, particularly with their emphasis on sustainable, local and ethical ingredients. As we saw in the previous chapter, there's a move away from waste and towards using less 'luxury' parts of animals and even plants.

by the way. Rather, small winemaking is a philosophical and aesthetic approach and is wrapped around concepts like using less, if any, chemicals, and taking care of the vines so they don't over produce, which can affect fruit quality and the life span of a grapevine.

Wineries that are big, medium or small can all employ a small winemaking ethos, one that is linked directly to the ground and the vines. The kinds of wines that result are a good fit for a restaurant – they're more crafted, as opposed to being made for mass consumption, and therefore have interesting characteristics that place them well with food. And this is a reason, right here, why restaurants are such an exciting place to not only drink wine but learn about it. You'll get to see real diversity in grape variety, regions, vineyards and style. It's a bit like chocolate, which we all like, right? Generic mass-made chocolate is all well and fine, addressing cravings and making you feel good. But eat a piece of artisanal chocolate with a high cocoa butter content, made with cocoa from a particular plantation in a particular growing region, and you'll notice the difference. It will make you sit up and pay attention. It will be more interesting and exciting than that mass-produced stuff – it will be memorable and special. And that's where food and wine are heading in the restaurant arena, right now: towards a more considered, quality approach to consumption.

The magic of good service

One of my favourite things in the world is to spend too much money in a restaurant, then walk out feeling it was worth every cent. A large part of what makes a restaurant experience so amazing is getting great service. And a big part of service is just basic, commonsense hospitality.

Once, I went to a birthday celebration at a family friend's home. I have an annoying tendency to be early and, true to form, I was knocking at his door 10 minutes before I was due. As he flung open the door and greeted me with a bear hug, the smell of roasting lamb was everywhere. Music was playing in the background. He took my jacket, thrust a glass of Champagne into my hand and warmly said, 'Welcome!' I walked into his dining room and saw how beautifully the table was set – such thought and attention had gone into everything – and I was fascinated by the way his simple acts of hospitality made me feel. A good restaurant should have the same approach at heart; they should be welcoming, hospitable and show a concern for the comfort of their guests. They shouldn't feel aloof or impenetrable.

WINE NOTE

I talk a lot about the sommelier's 'tasting toolkit'. The tools are not the thousands of flavours and aromas that are found in wine and food. Rather, they are the simple tastes and textures that connect food and wine. When you understand these tools and use them the right way, they can act like a 'blueprint' for your restaurant experience. What's good about this is that you can take it home with you and use it there, too. If you are cooking and entertaining at home, this tasting toolkit can be applied to whatever you are eating and drinking. So even though we are focusing on what happens in a restaurant, the information isn't exclusive to that particular experience.

I love service. I love working the dining room floor of a restaurant and, after nearly two decades of it, experience has taught me that it's the most visceral, engaging, dynamic and enjoyable place for people to enjoy wine.

The best example of service I've experienced was at The French Laundry, Thomas Keller's iconic restaurant in Yountville, California. We'd driven from Healdsburg, about an hour away, and our hire car had almost run out of petrol by the time we arrived. Our car was parked for us by the valet, then we were led to the dining room and seated at our table. What followed was just magical.

There's a saying that talks about the best service being the 'service you don't see', and the staff here were practically invisible, yet somehow everything was taken care of before we thought to ask. My wife and I kept saying that the way the floor team moved was like they were choreographed. (We only learned later that Thomas Keller had a history of employing dance instructors to teach wait staff how to move and engage with guests.) After the meal I went to pay, intending to leave a fairly solid tip. Not knowing the area, I asked directions to the nearest petrol station to fuel up our car. The maître d' handed me the car keys and simply said, 'It's been taken care of, sir, with our compliments'. He had heard about our fuel plight and decided to act on it. Now, in the interest of full disclosure, I have to say our booking was made by a former employer of mine, who knew the owner. Regardless, we were gob smacked, especially when the maître d' wouldn't let us reimburse the restaurant for the gas. Needless to say, that tip I left was mega-big. Was the restaurant's gesture one of care? Was it a gambit to ensure that huge tip? To be honest, I didn't care; I simply felt looked after and that was some of the best money I have ever spent in a restaurant.

These two experiences are both very different, but they speak to exactly the same thing. Namely, that service and hospitality are really just about caring for needs. As a sommelier I'm a big part of this equation so, to me, integral to the whole wine experience are gestures like offering a handshake, hanging a coat, smiling warmly and asking genuinely about a customer's day. The French word 'restaurant' has its roots in the word *restaurer*, which means to 'restore' or to 'refresh'. THAT, to me, should be at the very heart of a restaurant experience, whether I'm the one giving the service, or the one on the receiving end of it. Collectively, I think we are getting better at expecting hospitable service, and restaurants are certainly raising the bar across the board when it comes to offering it. More and more, polished service is an integral part of the whole dining-out package and has an immense impact on the quality of your restaurant experience.

'I' and 'my' versus 'you' and 'your'

You know when a sommelier is doing their job. It's when you start to do all the talking and they are simply listening. It's easy to recognise. Try this the next time you want to order wine in a restaurant and are asking for a recommendation. Count how many times the sommelier says 'I' or 'my' to you. As in, 'I love this wine', or 'This is my favourite grenache'. At the same time, note how many times they use the word 'you', as in, 'What wines do you normally like to drink?' or,

'What are you eating tonight, and would you like a wine specifically to go with it?' Of course, if you ask, 'What do you recommend?' the sommelier will logically go down the 'I' or 'my' path. You have invited them to do so. But if you haven't, they should be defaulting to 'you'. It demonstrates hospitality and an understanding that, for many diners, a wine list can be both exciting and terrifying. The 'you' demonstrates a desire to make you feel more comfortable and in control; for a diner, wine should not be a scary subject.

The 'you' approach does two very important things:

1. It gets you thinking, talking and starting to articulate what you want in a wine.
2. It gives the sommelier the information they need to select the correct wine for you.

Of course, in the end, you might just be happiest saying, 'I've got no idea what wine to choose. You're the expert, what do you recommend?' And that's OK, too. Sometimes customers are a bit taken aback when a sommelier drinks a little of the wine they've just ordered. Rest assured, though, they're not guzzling it. It's only ever about 10 ml ($^1/_4$ fl oz), which is 2 teaspoons. The sommelier trying your wine is actually an insurance policy for you; they will notice if something is not quite right with the wine and will certainly detect any faults in it that you may not recognise.

The wine list

Before we start talking specifically about wine lists, I want to be clear. 'Value' in wine is a relative concept and it doesn't mean 'cheap'. A $1000 wine can be a bargain and a $10 wine can be overpriced. I reserve a special type of loathing for wine lists formatted with individual wines listed in order of price, from cheapest at the top to the most expensive at the bottom. Within this system there is little significance given to a wine's origin or provenance. It doesn't take into account the food or the menu layout. It simply assumes that you will only rate a wine's quality by how much it costs. A great wine experience is so much more than the cost of a single bottle of wine. The further you progress on your journey in wine, the more your perception of value will change.

What you have probably realised, if you eat out regularly, is that wine lists are all different in layout, pricing, format and content. Most will have wines from grapes and regions that you can't pronounce, and you can't begin to guess what they may taste or smell like. Wine lists should have a clear connection with the food firstly. It doesn't necessarily need to be culturally connected (Italian wines with Italian food, for example), although this approach can help if the menu is traditional in some way.

If you're fearful of navigating a wine list – I can't tell you the number of times I have registered anxiety on a diner's face as I strode towards them with the wine list), it helps to remember this: it's really just a mass of numbers and letters on a piece of paper. It needs a human to bring it to life. The idea of good wine service is to make a very big world feel extremely small and personal. A large part of the value in a wine list is not in its actual content but in the person standing behind it. If you are in a place where the wine

WINE NOTE

Many writers and commentators love to take a swing at restaurants over their wine margins. They'll compare the price of a wine on a restaurant wine list to what it costs to buy in a bottle shop. Then they'll insinuate that the customer is somehow being ripped off. What they aren't accounting for is that wine mark-ups in a restaurant help to pay for wages, utilities, glassware, laundry, upkeep of the venue, investment in the business and the cost of buying food and wine. The question should be not how high someone marks up their wines, but where the value of a wine experience sits within a restaurant's business model. I see wine as an integral part of a restaurant experience and its pricing should be in balance with the menu.

WINE NOTE

I have a weak spot for riesling. As a result, most of the wine lists I have written or managed have large riesling sections. This doesn't mean they were boring – I built in plenty of diversity across regions, winemakers and price points. Because I loved this grape, I passed that passion on to the staff I worked with. When we would taste wines to see if they were good enough to be listed, we always took an extra few seconds with a riesling.

culture is strong and the staff is educated, use them. You'll get the best results if you are able to articulate what YOU like in a wine and are comfortable enough to be up-front about it. This doesn't mean that a sommelier runs off to find the exact wine you are describing, but they will at least know where to start. A good, clear, direct description of a wine from you can eliminate 90 per cent of the wine list immediately, which helps a lot, especially with large lists. If you are up for it, also let them know if you want to try something new. Most of the memories you will have around wine will be in those 'discovery moments', where you try something completely new for the very first time. But whether ordering some Old Faithful or stepping out of your wine comfort zone, everything will take its cue from your sense of taste.

HOW A WINE LIST IS STRUCTURED

Take a phone book – if you can still find one. It has thousands of pages but, if you know the surname and postcode of a particular person, you can find the right address in seconds. A good wine list works the same way. It has a set structure and, if you know where to look for things, you'll find the right wine really quickly. And it works the exact same way as a food menu does. In each, as you progress through them, both the food on a menu and the wine on a list will increase in weight, texture and mouthfeel. It's no accident that oysters, which are light-bodied, delicate, salty and creamy, are at the top of a menu. Likewise, if you read the top of the wine list, the first wines listed are the light-bodied and aromatic ones, such as Champagne and riesling. Flavour and body will continue to grow in concentration until you move through to the end, where the richest and most full-bodied foods and wines are located. On a menu, for example, these are generally red proteins like steak and slow-cooked meats, often teamed with powerfully flavoured sauces.

So ... if you like light, refreshing wines, look at the top or the beginning of the wine list. This is where you should find delicate, dry wines like sparkling wines and Champagne. White wines will be light-bodied varieties, represented by riesling, vermentino and pinot grigio. In this part of the list, the red selection will have wines with a lighter body, more acidity and softer tannins, such as gamay and pinot noir.

If you like medium-bodied, savoury wines, look in the middle section of a list. Writing a wine list for the contemporary wine drinker means more and more wines are falling into this category. This is because of their great versatility with food. Medium-bodied whites, such as sauvignon blanc, chenin blanc, semillon and pinot gris, and red varieties, such as nebbiolo, sangiovese, grenache and tempranillo, will fall here.

If you like bigger, rounder, full-bodied wines, go straight to the end of the wine list. Here you will find white wines loaded with more texture and fruit concentration. These whites will have increased levels of alcohol, and often oak, and will include varieties like roussanne, viognier and chardonnay. Red varieties follow a similar theme, with more texture, oak and increased levels of tannin – expect blockbusters like shiraz, merlot, cabernet and malbec.

When I first started judging restaurant wine lists for the Sydney Morning Herald Good Food Guide awards in

2007, I remember coming across a tightly structured wine list of 100 wines. It was at a new restaurant called Spice Temple, by legendary Australian chef and restaurateur Neil Perry. The food was modern Chinese and inspired by the provinces of Sichuan, Yunnan, Hunan, Jiangxi, Guangxi and Xinjiang. There were no cultural or historic defaults around this food as far as matching it with wine was concerned. The wine list had to be constructed in total deference to the food offered. Here, Perry's focus on light-bodied whites like riesling, and reds including gamay and pinot noir, showed respect for the heat and salt of many of the dishes. Medium-bodied and aromatic whites like pinot gris and gewürztraminer matched the various white proteins. Medium-bodied, low-tannin specimens like dolcetto and grenache matched the power and elegance of richer, red protein dishes. For me the real greatness of this list was how they tackled subject matter like full-bodied wines. They drew on acidity, not oak, for whites, particularly the chardonnay selection. The reds focused on elegance and freshness via cool-climate wines, rather than on the brute strength of warmer-climate reds with their oak, sweetness and alcohol. The result was a wine list that spoke to a unique menu that had no traditional footing, at all, with European-style dry wine.

THINGS TO CONSIDER WHEN CHOOSING WINE

When you're considering a wine list, it really helps if you know what you're not looking for, as much as what you are – even if you feel you don't know where to begin. Following are the key things to consider.

COLOUR

It may sound like a simplification but deciding on colour first will generally eliminate half the wine list immediately. By colour, I mean:

WHITE
ORANGE (WHITE WITH SOME SKIN CONTACT)
AMBER (WHITE WITH EXTENDED SKIN CONTACT)
PINK (ROSÉ)
RED

BODY

Considering body adds real 'weight' to the conversation and means you can weed out even more wines. It helps you narrow down the wine selection in a way that's meaningful to food.

LIGHT-BODIED
Choose this type if you are looking for fresh, cleansing, delicate wines.
MEDIUM-BODIED
Choose one of these if you are looking for more body and texture in a wine.
FULL-BODIED
Go here if you want wine with real depth and power.

TASTE AND TEXTURE

This is where you can add even more depth to your dialogue with a sommelier. Around these concepts you'll find words that you can use in a really useful way.

If you like a REFRESHING and CRISP wine, what you're actually looking for is ACIDITY.

If you like SAVOURY or GRIPPY wines, you're looking for wine with TANNIN.

If you like JUICY or FRUITY wines, you're after something with FRUIT CONCENTRATION.

Remember to focus on the characteristics here that you most enjoy – and remember you can like more than one of these. Regardless of the size of the wine list you're handed, these simple statements can cut out many of the 'wrong' wines from all the possible options.

SPECIALISATION

As you read through a wine list, you may see a particular narrative start to develop. The sommelier who wrote that list might have deep connections to a particular country, region, winemaker or style and this can come through in their list. Specialising can indicate investment in money and resources so quality and value should be high. Look for themes such as:

WINE AND SEAFOOD

Seafood requires similar considerations when it comes to wine selections. A menu anchored to light, delicate white proteins, shellfish and crustaceans requires a list with lighter, more subtle wines. White-centric lists should have a greater focus on light- to medium-bodied wine with acidity and freshness, and red-centric ones need to avoid high alcohol, sweetness and oak.

GRAPE VARIETY OR REGION

There will be a tighter selection of certain varieties or wines from specific regions. Any wine list with a focus on a particular grape variety will suggest that it's a passion project for the sommelier.

FEATURE PAGES

A wine list will often have a 'feature page', which is where a particular variety, region or winemaker has multiple wines listed, usually accompanied by a paragraph that gives some background and story to the wines. These mostly come out of tight relationships with particular winemakers.

FOOD AND WINE BIAS

Does the restaurant have a food 'bias'? This will reflect in the wine selection. For example, one restaurant group I worked for had a steak house and the majority of the dishes involved slabs of beef, pork and lamb. About 85 per cent of wines ordered were red and out of that, eight out of ten were either shiraz or cabernet sauvignon. It was no surprise, then, that we invested large amounts in reds generally, and shiraz and cabernet sauvignon specifically. We invested time, education and money into these kinds of wines as they worked with the food and hit a sweet spot for our customers.

In that same restaurant group, we had a wine bar where the menu was a mish-mash of cultural influences, ingredients and the customer base was younger – mostly drawn from creative services and advertising. As a consequence the list was diverse, and white and red wine sales were evenly split, and rosé was big business. The wine list was more wide-ranging in grape variety, region and wine style, with more blended wines than the steak house. So, expect wine 'bias' according to the menu of the place where you are dining. It's a good thing, though, showing thought and care in the food–wine synergy.

Communicating effectively

In my work in restaurants, I train service staff in the best methods to communicate effectively about wine. I get them to taste a wine, then formulate three key tasting-note style points about it. It's a simple process and one that you can use, too, to create 'one liner' statements that best describe your own wine tastes. These statements will not only help you whittle down choices when you want the right wine at home, but will also give a sommelier the kind of information they need to find the right wine for you at a restaurant. It's a process of deduction. The kinds of words that might get used could ultimately lead you to a statement such as this:

'I really like light-bodied, dry whites, especially with crisp fruit flavours and no oak. I am looking for a wine that would go with the oysters.'

How many pieces of information are there in this sentence?

'I really like the light-bodied (1) dry (2) white (3) wines with a crisp (4) and refreshing mouthfeel (5). I am looking for a wine that would go with the oysters (6).'

At this point, if a sommelier starts to talk to you about the flavours of wild strawberries and the aromas of crushed ants (seriously, some of them do), they have forgotten about you and are thinking of themselves. Reaffirming this approach should, in theory, bring them back to you and the moment. (Always remember, it's not about them.)

As a guest in a restaurant, trotting out your statement is the moment you should come to a fork in the road with your sommelier. I say 'should' because, unless you have a wine already in mind that you are utterly determined to drink, no decisions have been made yet about a wine selection. About now, the sommelier should present you with a couple of options based around your statement. One of these should be a 'safe' one – a wine that perfectly fits the 'brief' you have just given about your tastes. The other should lead you somewhere a little different, in which case your statement is only a starting point for an expanded horizon. You should always retain the option to choose which path to take, but you should be presented with some intelligent choices. This is where your sommelier can offer real value and make your restaurant experience truly memorable, because they'll see precisely where you are coming from. Because of the wines they have access to, they'll be able to suggest something that will further enrich your wine experience.

Don't get me wrong. If you insist on drinking a big, warm-climate shiraz with your oysters, then my job is just to fetch that wine and get it into your glass, quick smart. That's your prerogative. I'm hoping, though, that you wouldn't choose that route. And always remember that

The first 15 minutes of a dining experience are my favourite by far. I love anticipating what's to come ...

the wine industry has maybe the highest concentration of bullshit of any industry in the world. That's why, often, it's associated with convoluted language and so much pretension in the minds of many. The way a good sommelier speaks should be the way any good winemaker will speak – using direct, clear language. You rarely hear winemakers lapse into floweriness. When they talk about their wines they NEVER start with price point or marketing campaign, or even the flavours and aromas. They'll say things like what kind of year they had, what characteristics went into the wine, what vineyards or regions a wine is from and what the variety is. And they say it all very, very simply.

It's amazing how much information you can convey in a short amount of time, over a quick exchange. You just need to tweak what you convey, to reflect your level of curiosity, your knowledge and (importantly) what you are planning to eat.

The first 15 minutes – the aperitif

The first 15 minutes of a dining experience are my favourite by far. I love anticipating what's to come and the way you can read volumes into the quality of a restaurant from those vital first impressions. The Aperitif Moment should set the mood for the meal and the occasion around it. It should also set up your palate. High in acidity and often carrying bitterness to some degree or another, the pre-dinner drink is designed to spark your appetite. A good aperitif should make you think of food, and acidity is the key to this. Think of dry sherry, Champagne or vermouth. All these drinks are acknowledged as go-to pre-dinner drinks. Despite each having unique personalities and different points of origin, they all share one thing in common: high natural acidity. Let's look at a few.

MANZANILLA SHERRY This is purpose-built to go with those salty, oily snacks (white anchovies, olives, raw cured ham) that we all love to begin a meal with. Full of high natural acidity and with a distinctive, salty tang, dry sherry makes you salivate and practically lust for food.
DRY SPARKLING WINE Avoid drinking sugary, sweet bubbly before you eat. Sugar fogs up your palate, reducing your perception of taste, flavour and aroma. Choose sparkling wines that are crisp and dry.
DRY VERMOUTH Best served over ice, vermouth is a wine-based aperitif and perfect for those who like a little bitterness, a taste that is an effective stimulant for the appetite.

Wine by the glass

In a multi-course scenario, choosing wines by the glass allows a sommelier to really flex their muscles and create a very tailored wine experience for you. And it allows you to taste across an entire wine list. A good restaurant or wine bar should have a strong by-the-glass selection. When ordering wine by the glass, you can, and should, ask to taste it first. It's still wine out of a bottle after all, and you have every right to check it. It's unlikely the wines won't be in good condition, though I know people can have concerns on this score. Wines by the glass can come from bottles that have been opened for days – particularly more expensive ones that don't sell so often. But innovations in wine preservation have come a long way and the risk of spoiled wines is negligible these days. That said, a good

Pouring wine at the table is actually a big part of the overall wine experience and it's a great learning tool, too.

sommelier should be checking these wines every day and should absolutely let you taste.

Wine by the glass should be poured at the table. This isn't just a trust issue (although getting the wrong wine can make a huge difference in its price). Pouring wine at the table is actually a big part of the overall wine experience and it's a great learning tool, too. Just as they would if you had ordered the whole bottle, the sommelier should present the bottle to you and read back the label details (vintage, year, variety).

This is all good information that you can use to connect a particular wine back to a region and variety, and seeing the bottle makes this tangible. Store that information away, add it to your general knowledge and let it contribute to building your sensory memory.

Decanting

During most of the winemaking process, wine is shielded from oxygen. Oxidation (see page 136) is a common wine fault, which was more of an issue when wines were sealed under cork. In the screw-cap era, wines are fresher and more aromatic as oxygen doesn't get much of a look-in once the bottle is sealed. Oxygen, though, becomes part of wine's story when it's served and can add to the enjoyment of any wine. We add oxygen through decanting and, if you are ordering a wine by the bottle, always ask for it to be decanted. Why?

1. Opening a wine to let it breathe in the bottle is a complete myth. The only part of the wine that will breathe in this scenario is the small, coin-sized portion at the top, as nothing else has any exposure to air. Decanting, on the

other hand, circulates air through the wine rapidly and begins the process of oxidation, which, in the context of serving, is a good thing.

2. Decanting removes sediment and other solids from the wine, which are completely undesirable to drink.

3. Decanting gets a wine to its peak 'drinking window' quickly, thanks to that shot of oxygen. 'Reading' this window – which is one of the unique skills of a sommelier – is part science, part instinct, and it's taken me years to develop the intuition required to read a wine properly in this regard. (See page 230 for more information on the drinking window.)

Comfortable discovery

One of the great things about wine is how it has the ability to transport you, in terms of both time and place. When I drink gamay, for example – a light, juicy red wine – it reminds me of salami sandwiches and TGV train rides through France. A chilled glass of Sancerre, France's most famous sauvignon blanc, reminds me of scoffing fish and chips at the London restaurant I worked in. The salty intensity of Greek white wine reminds me of the heat and evening breezes of Crete. The taste of sherry sends me back to the wine bar in Melbourne where I started to fall in love with my wife.

Discovering new grape varieties is a real joy, but diving headlong into a new variety or country of origin can be scary when you don't have any reference points. You need to forgo familiar tastes and aromas and risk something new, but sometimes getting out of our wine comfort zone is a real challenge.

Some countries blend indigenous grape varieties with more internationally recognised ones like sauvignon blanc, merlot, cabernet and grenache, rendering them more approachable, and these blends can be a less risky way into a new realm of wine. (See Blended wines, page 51.) There can be real barriers, though, when you're looking at wines from a variety or region you have no experience with. The main ones are:

1. PRONUNCIATION
If it's a tongue twister (try saying vergelegen or Bourgueil or cserszegi fuszeres), this is an impediment. Many people don't want to go through the embarrassment of pronouncing it incorrectly.

2. COMPARISON
If it's hard (or even impossible) to compare an unknown wine with a variety you may already know and understand, you're unlikely to go there.

As more countries enter the global wine market, they all bring with them unique grapes and regions. When considering an unfamiliar grape, I always suggest people look for blended iterations that feature that particular variety. For example, on page 175 I mention the gum-numbing red wines made from the xinomavro grape. These are super-high in acidity and tight, grippy tannins; it's an acquired taste. However, add some merlot, with its fruitiness and low tannins, or syrah with its spice, alcohol, fruit sweetness and colour, and xinomavro is transformed

into a softer, more rounded wine. The blended wine will taste less of xinomavro, while still allowing you some understanding of it. It's a far less risky way into this particular wine.

Just like travel, wine provides a powerful way to visit unknown places, and restaurants are integral to this process. Restaurants can curate global collections built on hard-to-source wines from all over the place, giving you the chance to taste wines you wouldn't normally access. If there are countries you haven't visited, then wines from those areas are a wonderful way to get real insights into them. And a good sommelier can guide you through this potentially fraught experience by recommending blends as a lower risk way to go.

Country of origin

Restaurants have always acted like ambassadors for certain cuisines and cultures. Food in a restaurant setting has arguably done more to spread the cultural message of countries like France, Italy and Spain in recent years than art, music or literature have.

As we've seen, not all countries have a complementary food/wine tradition, but on the following pages is a chart listing some of the best known that do.

INTERNATIONAL WINE

SPAIN

Perhaps no country has had more influence over the way we eat in restaurants in recent times than Spain. Despite the creativity and innovation in Spanish food, the real beauty of its culinary culture is – for me anyway – in the way everyone can eat well at any price. Tapas and short-course eating are at the heart of this, and the dynamic, powerful flavours that swirl around these dishes (anchovies, cured meats, olives, cheeses, spices like smoked paprika and so on) cry out for wine. Some key wines to look for include:

VERDEJO FROM RUEDA A light-bodied, dry, fruity, soft, super 'smashable' (see page 68) white wine – good as an aperitif or as a lighter wine for lunch.

ALBARINO FROM RÍAS BAIXAS Medium-bodied white. Can be varied in style depending on the producer. It will range from light and savoury, to full-flavoured and textured.

TXAKOLI (ALSO SPELLED CHACOLÍ) FROM THE BASQUE COUNTRY (GREEN WINE) This is the locals' wine. This white wine can be dry or lightly sparkling but, either way, it's clean, bone-dry and rippling with acidity. It's a wine designed to counter salty, oily snacks.

MENCÍA FROM THE BIERZO, RIBEIRA SACRA AND VALDEORRAS REGIONS Light- to medium-bodied, spicy, savoury and a nice transition wine between light-bodied and full-bodied red. It's very versatile.

TEMPRANILLO Best examples are from the regions Rioja and Ribera del Duero in northern Spain. Medium to full-bodied red wine.

FRANCE

A great deal of the wine we drink today in countries such as Australia, South America, New Zealand and the USA have their roots in French vineyards. And in French, or French-inspired kitchens, generations of chefs have learned about the importance of regionalism and provenance. Food and wine are literally part of the French DNA. Below are a few of the wines I have come to know over the years. No tricks or twists here, just flat-out drinkability and very high quality.

MELON DE BOURGOGNE FROM MUSCADET A light-bodied white of delicious contrasts. Creamy, crisp and subtle, it's produced in the Loire Valley.

WHITE BLENDS FROM THE RHÔNE VALLEY Medium-bodied, textural, fruity, full-flavoured and fresh white. There is literally an entire fruit salad of grapes that can be used for these wines. They are great alternatives if you like white wines with punch, but you're tired of chardonnay. Try viognier, marsanne, roussanne (great individually, but better together in a blend) and grenache blanc.

CHARDONNAY FROM CHABLIS Light to medium-bodied, precise, tense and high-acid white wines that have little or no oak. Once you've had a good bottle of Chablis, it will become the kind of white that makes you salivate when you think of it.

GAMAY FROM BEAUJOLAIS Probably the most underrated wine from France. Light, crisp and almost crunchy in texture with a supple juiciness. If you like light-bodied French red but don't want to pay the high prices of red Burgundy, this is your wine.

CABERNET FRANC FROM THE LOIRE VALLEY Medium-bodied, dark, aromatic red with firm, chalky tannin. Another cracking alternative French red for those not willing to salary-sacrifice for a bottle of Bordeaux.

INTERNATIONAL WINE

INTERNATIONAL WINE

ITALY

Perhaps no other country has the origins of its wines so closely woven into the history of its food as Italy. The idea of serving food and wine at the table together goes back to the Roman Empire. However, Italy has really come into its own as a producer of quality wine, at all levels, since the middle of the twentieth century. Either delicate or powerfully flavoured, rustic or refined, Italian food has a connection to its origins and its producers that few other countries can match.

VERMENTINO FROM SARDINIA Crisp, zesty, chalky dry with long lines of tingly acidity. A great aperitif-style dry white.

GARGANEGA FROM SOAVE Gets the award for most improved wine in Italy. What was once brownish, cloying and often oxidised, is now a medium-bodied, supple and crackling white with freshness on the back palate.

PECORINO FROM ABRUZZO Medium-bodied red with a slightly more rounded palate feel. Can get a little high in alcohol, which can give the wine a softer mouthfeel, but its high natural acidity balances it.

SANGIOVESE FROM CHIANTI Medium-bodied, super savoury and fresh red wine, and the cornerstone of Italian wine lists for centuries. Wines from the region of Chianti are responsible for some of the best, and worst, wines ever made in Italy. Many of sangiovese's faults have been eliminated by more care in both the vineyard and winery by winemakers and growers.

NEBBIOLO FROM LANGHE OR ALBA Food loves it. This red is sexy with an almost more-ish drinkability, and a versatility that can suit any occasion. It's like wine's version of a Swiss army knife. Langhe and Alba are the entry level regions for nebbiolo in its home region of Piedmont in Italy's northwest.

GREECE

There is so much emotion and honesty in Greek food
and wine. With a new group of winemakers and grape
growers coming through, the future of Greek wine is
being addressed in a very different way from previous
generations. One of the fascinating things about Greece
is that nearly 90 per cent of all its grape varieties are
indigenous and unique to Greece. This is a country to
watch over the coming years.

ASSYRTIKO FROM SANTORINI Postcard-perfect backdrops are
nothing new to the winemaking fraternity of Santorini. What is changing,
though, is the growing demand from sommeliers and wine buyers for
this light- to medium-bodied dry white, crackling with acidity and a dry,
savoury mouthfeel.

MALAGOUSIA FROM MACEDONIA AND ATTICA Medium- to full-
bodied white wine that can be as bold as chardonnay in texture and
mouthfeel. Oak adds to the wine's complexity and richness. It should be
drunk young and shouldn't be overly chilled.

XINOMAVRO FROM NAOUSSA This red is the king of wine in northern
Greece. Wines can vary from light- to medium-bodied and savoury, to
fuller bodied, dense, astringent wines with deep, dark flavours and
gum-numbing tannins.

AGIORGITIKO FROM THE PELOPONNESE Greece's most successful
red variety – pronouncing this wine makes you feel like you have a
mouth full of marbles. The dense, fruity, softly textured wines are
consistent and eminently drinkable.

INTERNATIONAL WINE

Countries with no wine heritage: matching wine and food

A great many countries have popular cuisines that share no history with wine. While they have great food, they've mainly got climates that are unsympathetic to growing grapes and, for that reason – and others to do with, perhaps, society and religion – wine has never really caught on. However, the techniques, influences and flavours behind nearly any kind of food, no matter what its culinary origins, can find an empathetic wine partner.

This is an interesting topic and one that could be the subject of another entire book. The chart that follows is a potted discussion only, loosely based around a few major cuisines, designed to get you thinking. The underlying fundamentals of the approach to wine I've laid out for you here, can, in theory, be applied to absolutely any dish from any cuisine. This is not going to provide you with a definitive set of charts or 'this goes with that' guidelines. I'd encourage you to start thinking about your favourite cuisine, and wines for it, in the simplest of terms. (See also the chapters A matter of taste, and Matching food and wine for more information on pairing food with wine.)

THAILAND

Aromatic, salty, sweet, sour and spicy, Thai food is famous for its intensity of flavour and heat. There's both complexity and freshness in Thai food, from ingredients such as lime juice, herbs like mint, lemongrass and coriander (cilantro), sweet spices, chilli and the mellowing effects of coconut milk.

Wines that can handle the complexity of Thai cooking are ones that are un-oaked or have subtle oak character. They need to have lots of acidity and ripe, juicy fruit flavour too. Acidity and sweetness actually reduce your perception of heat. Light-bodied whites like riesling can have a flick of sweetness, which can temper the searing heat of chilli. Avoid high-tannin reds at all costs.

WHITE

Dry riesling from Eden Valley or Clare Valley, South Australia
Pinot gris from New Zealand
Sylvaner from Alsace, France

RED

Gamay from Beaujolais or the Savoie, France
Pinot noir from Mornington Peninsula, Australia
Dolcetto from Piedmont, Italy

INTERNATIONAL WINE

INTERNATIONAL WINE

SCANDINAVIA

These cold, northern climates close to the ocean produce dishes with pristine and pure characters. Scandinavian food, with its recurring theme of salt, oil, raw, cured and fermented, is well suited to wines that are light- to medium-bodied. High tannins or excessive sweetness in wine will smother the complexity, delicacy and refinement of Scandinavian food. Another group of wines that work well are those that have had skin contact (see page 139). Such wines are especially good with fermented and cured foods. Skin contact in white wine introduces soft tannins which, when partnered with a white wine's natural acidity, gives the wine an 'umami' character, or savoury taste (see page 94). This umami character is also a feature of fermented foods and, when combined with the right wines, they meld into each other.

WHITE

Riesling from Pfalz or Rheinhessen, Germany, or Eden Valley, South Australia

Assyrtiko from Santorini, Greece

SKIN-CONTACT WHITE

Chardonnay from Jura, France

Chinuri from Georgia

RED

Gamay from Savoie, France

Nebbiolo from Piedmont, Italy

Trousseau from Jura, France

KOREA

When I think of Korean food I think of barbecue, hot pots, salty fermented kimchi, the powerful flavours of meaty stocks and the spice-hit of gochujang, or Korean red chilli paste. Korean flavours are big and so are the textures. Wines for Korean barbecue should have guts and grip; there are loads of savoury, smoky flavours present, while hot pots require fruit concentration but softer tannins. Staple Korean dishes, such as soups and hot pots, usually have good levels of fat, so wines with a high natural acidity, which will cut this, suit best. Avoid any wine with high tannin levels – tannin will amplify heat, making spicy food taste like someone has stuck a flame thrower in your mouth.

WHITE
Dry riesling from Australia
Sweet riesling from Germany (if the food is high in spice)
Pinot gris from New Zealand
Sauvignon blanc from New Zealand

RED
Young gamay from France
Grenache from Australia
Red blends of grenache, shiraz and mourvèdre, France
Malbec from Argentina
Barossa or McLaren Vale shiraz from Australia

INTERNATIONAL WINE

MEXICO

Mexican food is so much more than clichéd ideas around tacos, nachos and tortillas. A varied and highly regional cuisine, its flavours can be fresh and also hearty, warm and rustic. Complex sauces like mole, long-simmered meat and bean stews, simple grills, crunchy salads spiked with the fragrance of cumin, lime, coriander (cilantro), and a whole suite of chilli varieties, both fresh and dried, are just some of the hallmarks of the Mexican diet. It's a cuisine that does best with medium-bodied red wines that have firm, savoury tannins. The freshness of light- to medium-bodied white wines are perfect fits, too. Chilli heat is tempered by white and red wines with higher fruit concentration and greater texture. Avoid high-alcohol wines, as these not only dull and desensitise your palate, but they simply don't respond well to the earthy flavours in Mexican food.

WHITE
White blends from the southern Rhône Valley, France
Sauvignon blanc from New Zealand
Gewürztraminer from France
Dolcetto from Italy

RED
Zinfandel (primitivo) from the USA or Italy
Tempranillo from Rioja, Spain

JAPAN

There is such beauty and grace in Japanese food. I am a self-confessed sake nut and I see the same grace and elegance in sake as I do in the aesthetics, flavours and textures of Japanese food. There's a light freshness to this cuisine, with its emphasis on pristine seafood, and fleetingly available seasonal produce, picked at the peak of its perfection. With raw seafood, keep the wine light and fresh. With their high acidity, the wines below also work well with the delicate fats in tempura batter.

WHITE

Dry manzanilla sherry from Spain

Dry sparkling wine from Burgundy, France, or Tasmania, Australia

Riesling from Mosel, Germany

Pinot blanc and pinot gris from Alsace, France

RED

Gamay from Beaujolais, France

Pinot noir from France

Barbera from Italy

Cabernet franc from France

INTERNATIONAL WINE

Just because a type of wine is popular, or other people you know like it, it doesn't mean you should too.

Passionfruit or cat's pee?

If you and I have the same wine in the same circumstances, we will both draw different things from it. If we both drink a glass of sauvignon blanc, for example, you might get the legendary passionfruit and pineapple notes, while I might just get cat's pee. And that's OK. I believe there is no such thing as objectivity in wine; everything is skewed, in some measure, to personal preference. Just because a type of wine is popular, or other people you know like it, it doesn't mean you should too.

That's what I like about the dining room floor. It's a mosh pit of varying tastes, budgets, preferences and belief systems around food and wine. Everyone is so different; the sommelier's job is to find you the right wine, every time. Who knows, you might also learn something along the way.

SERVING WINE
AT HOME

Having wine knowledge should be non-apparent when it comes to applying it in a practical way. Your knowledge can be deep and well honed but it should take a back seat to what is ultimately the purpose of wine – to share and enjoy. If I serve you in a restaurant, you shouldn't be aware of all my learning, experience and skill. You should just be aware of my simple acts – asking how your day was, bringing you a bottle of wine, opening it for you and filling your glass. It works the same way in your home, where the service of wine should come across as easy. But behind it, there should still be preparation, where the things your guests don't see are as important as the things they do see. In this spirit, what follows are a few of my tips for serving wine at home, and a few different scenarios for serving different types of wines. Above all, when you have people over and there's wine drinking on the agenda, you need to be prepared, with everything organised. I've developed a simple routine and the following are the main aspects of this.

Your knowledge can be deep and well honed but it should take a back seat to what is ultimately the purpose of wine — to share and enjoy.

Temperature

It goes without saying that some wines need to be served chilled and some don't. But wine temperature goes a little beyond this simplistic understanding. I love working with the temperature of wine. Changing it is one of the few ways you can effectively modify a wine. Wine arrives in a bottle as a Done Deal and, apart from decanting it and pairing it with food, there aren't too many ways you can change its fundamental characteristics. Playing with its temperature, though, can actually shift the texture and taste of a wine.

For example, if you slightly chill a full-bodied shiraz (even for 5 minutes), you can reduce the perception of its sweetness and alcohol and the wine will taste fresher. I think that, in general, white wines are consumed too cold and, if you warm them a touch, you release more of their flavour and aroma. A too-cold oaked chardonnay, for example, will just taste like oak. But if it is served a little warmer, the oak recedes and reveals more of the wine's true taste and fruit character. I liken modifying temperature in wine to using salt in cooking. A little here, a little there and you can augment flavours. It's a subtle tool, but one that's very effective.

Glassware

Here's what I know about glassware. It matters – but not as much as you might think it does. Does a wine glass that is specifically designed to accentuate the delicate structure and intense aromatics of pinot noir express those characteristics in greater intensity than if the wine was served in a paper cup? Science and a lot of wine 'experts' will say yes. But will you enjoy it more? Well, of that I am not so sure.

Glassware for me is more about an occasion-based idea, rather than a wine-based one. If you're drinking outside for instance, at a picnic or a barbecue, it's likely the food served will be light and fresh. Meats cooked over a fire, served with accompaniments like bread and salad, tend to be served casually on disposable plates. Wines consumed in the same scenario should fit with the easy going, undemanding nature of the occasion. I'd pour them into plastic cups – fine

WINE NOTE

I have lost count of the number of friends who have told me stories of their travels to other countries, where their fondest memory is of a time they grabbed a local bottle of wine from a wine shop, bundled it up with some meat, cheese and bread, and consumed it all on some hillside or by a river, sometimes even slugging the wine straight from the bottle! Not that I encourage you to do that, of course. But not having access to the right glassware was hardly a deterrent to the proper enjoyment of the wine.

glassware or crystal is just a nightmare outside, or in any situation where you need to transport them, unless you're a professional caterer. Plastic cups are a no-brainer.

In contrast, the ceremony of a formal, sit-down-dress-up dinner requires a sprinkling of theatre and magic. Fine glassware, which looks as if it would shatter the moment you coughed near it, is the call here. A great deal of this type of glassware is designed specifically for a single grape variety, which makes sense considering the kinds of wines served in this environment are at the pointy end of the quality spectrum, and will respond well to bespoke glassware.

When entertaining at home, I tend to stick to a casual dining/casual glassware, formal dining/formal glassware formula. If I'm having a 'proper' dinner party and friends are bringing special wines, I definitely make an effort with glassware – and the table setting, generally. But if not, then it's casual all the way. You don't need a gaggle of varietal-specific glasses either, by the way, to entertain well at home. These are nice but a set each of decent white and red wine glasses is all you need. But make sure they are good quality and that you have enough so you don't get caught washing them halfway through a dinner, if your white or red changes direction. Good glasses are nicer to handle and they do make wine look more special than cheap ones.

You need to properly prepare your glassware before serving wine. Even if they look clean, they still likely need some attention. Here are a couple of cleaning techniques I find indispensable before I serve any wine.

STEAM CLEANING

This is the best way to remove streaks from glassware – hold up any glass to the light, no matter how clean you think it is, and you'll probably see streaks. They need to go before you use those glasses, and steaming is the best way. Steam cleaning can also get rid of what, in the industry, we call 'box taint'. If you're using glasses that have been stored in cardboard boxes for a while, they start to get a certain musty smell. The risk is, if you pour wine into them, that mustiness can be transferred to it. So, to get rid of streaks and any box taint, pour boiling water into a bucket, to create plenty of steam. Hold each glass, upside down, over the steam and let it fill the glass. Use a clean, dry cloth to immediately dry off the inside of the glass and remove every last bit of water (which could later dilute the wine). Streaks and taint will be gone. I like this cleaning method as it's both effective and chemical-free. Residues of cleaning detergents inside wine glasses are very undesirable as they too can taint your wine.

SEASONING

This is where you take a little of the wine that you are about to serve and pour it into one of your serving glasses. Then, you swirl it around so it lightly coats the inside of the glass, pour the remaining wine into another glass and repeat this process until all the glasses you are about to use have been 'seasoned'. Any wine that remains afterwards I pour back into the bottle or decanter. Or drink. It's usually such a small quantity that it's not going to affect wine in a full bottle or decanter. Seasoning helps prepare a glass for the wine, and also removes any minute traces of impurities in the glass that you might not have picked up through steaming. It's a fun thing to do too and a great opportunity to perfect your swirling technique. I learned about seasoning from Italian sommeliers in London – they always did this prior to wine service. It's an old-world technique but still appropriate.

Decanting

The characters in wine we discuss at length in this book are ones that are not only compatible with food but are also incredibly responsive to, and easy to modify with, oxygen. I'm sure you've heard someone say, 'I will just open the wine to let it breathe'. But, truthfully, if you let a wine sit around with its cork or screw-top off, the only part of it actually exposed to oxygen is an area about the size of a small coin. It's the equivalent of you breathing through a straw and hoping to get sufficient oxygen – it simply won't happen. You need to get the whole wine exposed to air, and decanting achieves this quickly.

Tannin, for example, is a red wine's most powerful natural antioxidant. By using a decanter and aerating a wine, a chain reaction begins where oxygen (aeration caused by decanting) and antioxidants (tannins) in a red wine take each other on. This causes tannins to appreciably soften. Then there's alcohol. While you can't reduce the alcohol percentage of a wine through decanting, you can lower your perception of it. High alcohol is registered as a smell similar to the type you find in hard white spirits like vodka. Wine isn't a spirit and shouldn't smell like one. Decanting will give these aromas a chance to 'blow off' and dissipate. It will also help integrate the alcohol into the wine by softening tannins and encouraging fruit flavours to the fore. This is all the work of oxygen and I can't stress enough how decanting improves any and every wine. As well as aeration, the historical purpose of decanting was to remove sediment. Thanks to modern winemaking practices, sediment is not an issue in most' entry-level wine today, but it is with more 'interesting' wines made according to small winemaking principles, where winemakers are actually filtering their wines less and less. 'Offcuts' like skins, stalks and lees tend to be left in contact with these sorts of wines for a longer period, and not ironed out with filtration prior to bottling. So in those wines, sediment could well be more in evidence.

Decanting can act like a flashlight on any potential wine faults. If you think there may be a fault with a wine (any unpleasant aroma, taste or texture), then exposing the wine to oxygen by decanting it will reveal these problems and do it much quicker than if you are simply tasting it in a glass.

A decanter can, in theory, be anything, but some shapes are more effective than others. What kind of vessel you use is largely to do with how much you invest personally in wine. If you like easy-drinking plonk, then a glass jug will do. Are you an avid collector with special wines put away? Then you might want to invest in a cut-crystal decanter worth hundreds of dollars. It's really up to you. In general terms, I like a decanter with a narrow neck and wider base, which comfortably fits in the palm of my hand – you want a broad-based one as the wider the base, the more of the wine will

WINE NOTE

Actually, I'm not a huge fan of fancy decanters. Yes, they add a sense of theatre to wine service in upmarket restaurants, but for home use, a simple, solid decanter is best. There's no added functionality that comes with these ornate decanters; they don't make your wine taste any better.

be exposed to air, thus accelerating the effects that oxygen will have on the wine. How long a wine stays in the decanter really depends on the wine and, as we saw and you will need to keep tasting it to check how it is responding to oxygen (see Drinking window, page 230). Some wines will need hours in the decanter, others just a few minutes. Pour the wine into a decanter at a 45-degree angle and, pouring right against the opposite side of the decanter neck, allow the wine to follow the surface of the glass down into the base, so it doesn't froth as it hits the decanter.

CLEANING DECANTERS

When you use decanters a lot, especially with red wines, you'll start to notice a build up of colour from the wine on the base of your decanter. You might even notice bits of brown sediment sticking to it. Because of their narrow necks, decanters are notoriously hard to clean properly, especially the really arty, sculptural ones you can get.

You can buy specially designed brushes to clean a decanter, which look rather like something you would clean your toilet with. If you want a simple 'trade hack', the best way to clean a decanter is by using rock salt. Put a handful of it into your decanter, add a little water then swirl the decanter. The salt, which is abrasive, finely scratches the glass – these are microscopic scratches however, so don't worry as you can't see them. The salt acts a bit like fine sandpaper, removing impurities and stains and leaving your decanter crystal clean. Rinse the decanter well and be sure to drain out every last bit of water as any residue will dilute your wine.

Mise en place

If you're familiar with kitchen talk, you'll have heard of 'mise en place'. It's French for 'putting in place' and it's what every chef works to assemble before a kitchen opens for lunch or dinner service. If they don't have all their prep, or mise en place, done, a kitchen quickly descends into chaos once meal orders stream in. It's the same with wine service. Either in a restaurant or at home, being organised is really, really important. Nothing ruins a dinner party or other occasion more than lack of planning. That same effort you put into your menu (researching recipes, writing shopping lists, shopping and so on) should also go into choosing and serving your wines. Make sure you have enough glasses for each course, that your decanter(s) is sparkling clean and that you have other bits of your 'service tool kit' at the ready:

- A waiter's friend
- At least one good, clean cloth for catching wine dribbles as you pour
- Ideally a wine spout to prevent excess drips (I make my own using small plastic discs that I roll to form into a tube shape and pop into a bottle)
- Some muslin (cheesecloth) – if wines are aged or you want to remove the risk of sediment by straining them
- A funnel for decanting. Place it in the top of your decanter to prevent the wine from spilling and making it easier to decant.

Pouring wine

The idea of pouring a bottle of wine while holding it by the base is an old-school one. It developed as a technique so

WINE NOTE

If I had to write a training manual for wine service it would not start with wine. It would mainly be about deportment, how to speak, being respectful, having great manners and so forth. There has to be a genuine intent and connectivity with others at the heart of wine service, and this is as valid at home as it is in a restaurant.

a waiter or sommelier couldn't cover the label when they poured. This allowed the customer to check they were getting the wine they ordered while also reading any other information on the label. However, part of good wine service includes reading out the relevant information on the label to a guest prior to pouring. These days, though, there is less information on labels. Labels tend to be more a design feature than anything and they don't tell you much more than alcohol levels, where a wine is from and if it contains sulphites or not. I do think that pouring while holding a bottle by the base is more elegant than grabbing it around the neck but, really, you can hold it any way that feels comfortable; and according to what feels safe – a full wine bottle is very heavy. However you hold it, you might be interested in two fundamental courtesies that I still teach to staff when it comes to the pouring and serving of wine. These are: first, don't ever interrupt a conversation to pour wine and, second, never interrupt the line of sight between people to pour wine. I learned these from a very rigid French restaurant I worked in and although service is a bit more relaxed these days, I still think serving wine revolves around the practice of good manners and etiquette.

Serving wine outdoors

I remember commuting to work one day when I was living in London. It was literally the first day of summer and it seemed the entire city had undergone a personality transplant. People were smiling, not scowling. Everyone was suddenly in a good mood thanks to the shift in the weather (if you've been to London much, you'll know what I mean). Arriving at the restaurant to start my shift, I was greeted by the sight of the sommelier filling tubs with ice and dumping every bottle of chablis and Champagne we had in them, to chill. Warm weather in London means drinking light, refreshing wines and, sure enough, by the end of service we'd sold so much Chablis and Champagne we were desperately ringing suppliers to replenish stock. New seasons, specific moods, various times and places all demand different wines.

When it warms up, the outdoors beckons, allowing for relaxed alfresco dining. Food in outdoor settings tends to be light and the flavours bright. Salads, vegetables, meats, cheeses and breads are favoured, and wines should be in keeping with these and with the general informality attached to eating outside. Sparkling wines with refreshing acidity and a delicate texture and flavour are perfect. Whites and reds should veer to the light-bodied side and rosé is a sure-fire winner – it can be any shade of pink you like but try to avoid rosés that are overly sweet – sugar will drown out the fresh flavours of summery food. For pure food friendliness, the pale-coloured ones are the best; when made well, these have loads of refreshing, crisp tastes and textures that cut through oil, salt and light proteins like fish and chicken. (See the chapters A matter of taste, and Matching food and wine for more details on matching specific food with wine.)

PICNICS
Picnics are about simple, fresh and light food that you can eat with your hands. This kind of food needs wines with an equally uncomplicated nature. Being outdoors and in warmer temperatures generally means salads; light,

salty, oily vegetables (antipasto); simple meats (including charcuterie as well as cured and smoked meats and fish); maybe pies such as quiche; shellfish and crustaceans (oysters and prawns/shrimp); sandwiches and cheeses. Whether wines are white, pink or red, they should always be light, fresh, aromatic and refreshing. (See page 207 for a list of suggested wines for a picnic.)

BARBECUES

Where there's smoke there's flavour! The effect of fire on food hits such a sweet spot for all kinds of wines. Cooking over fire adds extra, robust flavours to meats, rendering fats and adding wonderful crunchy char. Wines with good texture, decent amounts of acidity and subtle, savoury tannins work particularly well with barbecued food, which, let's face it, is usually structured around thick bits of meat. Look for wines that have 'firm' mid-range tannins and acidity with higher concentrations of fruit. (See page 208 for a list of suggested wines for a barbecue.)

CHILLING RED WINE

If you can't tear yourself away from a full-bodied red habit, a good tip is to chill these for drinking on warm days, even for a few minutes. This will reduce your perception of sweetness and alcohol in the wine, making its taste fresher and more in tune with a casual occasion. Throw your reds into your esky or ice chest, where you are chilling other beverages, for a maximum of 5 minutes.

The key here is picking wines that are not too 'serious'. Dining among the heat and haze of an outdoor barbecue is not the place for single-vineyard shirazes from the Barossa Valley or for some precious Burgundy. Lighter, blended, easy-drinking wines are the optimal barbecue drink. There's a greater selection than ever before in this category of lighter, savoury wines. That goes for rosés, too. With their high acidity and smooth textures, rosés are well suited to outdoor entertaining – they look gorgeous in the glass as well. Remember that when people reach for a drink at these sorts of casual occasions, they're not very focused on what's in the bottle. Maybe after they taste a wine they'll ask, 'Oh wow, what's this?' but, in the main, they just want a glass in their hand soon after arriving and to get socialising. It's the same with picnics too. Particular wines and their pedigree are of less relevance to this sort of get together and you shouldn't select wines that are too serious. They'll get lost in the proceedings. (See the chapters A matter of taste, and Matching food and wine for more information on pairing.)

Dinner parties

Cooking for a group of your nearest and dearest is one of life's great joys. I love everything about hosting a dinner party – the planning, the shopping, the preparation of glassware, setting the table, the cooking and the anticipation of the doorbell ringing. I love cooking with wine and I always enjoy a good glass while I'm slaving over the stove – Sinatra blaring in the background. It's definitely one of my happy places.

When planning an event like this, first off you need to hit on an overall food approach, as this will affect the way you think about the wines. Will you be cooking something tried and trusted from your repertoire, that you know you can deliver easily and whose familiar flavours you feel confident you can easily match with wines? Or are you going to challenge yourself by making something completely new? Are you going with a country of origin (theming your meal, say Spanish, Italian or Thai)? Or will you shape your meal around some heroic piece of produce, such as a large whole fish, a lamb shoulder or a roast of beef rib-eye on the bone? Will the dishes be structured around a progression of courses, or served on big platters, family-style? The answers to these questions will help you consider what the appropriate wines are for the food, and the occasion. You might settle for 'easy'

BRING A BOTTLE

Guests generally want to contribute a bottle of wine to a dinner party, so it's a good idea to discuss the menu with them ahead of time so they can form an idea about what they might like to bring. This is rather like French food culture, and how so much of it is wrapped around the planning, shopping and preparing of a dish or dishes. The French love to talk about what they're planning to cook; it's a big part of their entire ethos around food. Getting yourself, and your guests, excited is such a big part of the process. Generally, I reckon the best dinner party wines are mouth-watering ones and not big, boozy, thickly textured ones.

wines, if that's reflected in your menu, or you might pull out all the stops with a few special bottles chosen from your cellar. It really all depends.

ARRIVAL

After working for so long in restaurants, I've had drilled into me the idea that when a guest arrives, they need to instantly be greeted, made comfortable and have the appropriate drink put in their hand within 30 seconds. I subscribe to this theory when entertaining at home. I make sure that before the doorbell rings I have glasses ready and sparkling, light snacks set up and the right wines at the ready, to get things off to a smooth start. You don't want to be dithering around with preparations when people arrive at the door. You want them to feel welcomed, and being organised helps in this. The ultimate welcome drink to my mind is non-vintage Champagne. It's a wine with a simplicity and freshness, yet lots of flavour. Vintage Champagnes are lovely but that extra time in the cellar makes them too intense and complex to drink on their own or with light snack food, I think. Remember that Champagne is just another wine – albeit a distinctive one – and has its rightful place with food, too. (See page 209 for a list of suggested 'welcome wines'.)

MULTIPLE SMALL COURSES

The older model of appetiser, main and dessert is more frequently being subverted into multiple, set-course dining in restaurants. It's a worthy way to go at home, too, when you are entertaining. It's an approach that creates opportunity for greater variations of flavour and texture across a menu, and opens up the number of wine styles you can drink as well. If you're cooking six or so small dishes, follow the restaurant rule by bringing out the lightest, most delicate dishes first and then build towards the heaviest, richest dishes to finish. Wine selections should share a similar theme: lighter and fresher to start, heavier and richer at the end.

EXAMPLE OF A WHITE-WINE PROGRESSION WITH SMALL DISHES:
LIGHT-BODIED
Riesling from Rheingau, Germany
MEDIUM-BODIED
Albarino from Rías Baixas, Spain
FULL-BODIED
Chardonnay from Margaret River, Western Australia

EXAMPLE OF A RED-WINE PROGRESSION WITH SMALL DISHES
LIGHT-BODIED
Pinot noir from Marlborough, New Zealand
MEDIUM-BODIED
Grenache from Barossa Valley, Australia
FULL-BODIED
Cabernet sauvignon from Bordeaux, France

LARGE COURSES

If you've based your menu around a particularly hefty main course (a large winter roast, a meat braise or a whole poached salmon, for example), you need wines that will 'cut'. By that I mean wines that aren't excessively sweet, or heavy with oak and alcohol. You need wines with good acidity and tannin that will help digestion. You also want plenty of the same wine in this scenario. Don't change the selection mid-course as you'll just confuse the overall wine/food message.

WINE IDEAS FOR LARGER COURSES

WHITE

Roussanne, albarino, fiano, chardonnay

RED

Sangiovese, dolcetto, nebbiolo, tempranillo

Wine service tips ('trade hacks')

Finally, there are a few wine service tips that I'd like to share with you, which I hope will be useful. Most 'trade hacks' are used during service, when problems arise with a wine that require a quick solution. Following are some troubleshooting solutions for the most common problems you are likely to be faced with when serving wine at home.

1. TAKING THE CHILLED EDGE OFF A BOTTLE OF TOO-COLD WINE

Empty the bottle of wine into a decanter. Next, fill a large bowl with hot water from the kitchen tap. Place the decanter in the heated water, ensuring the level of the water meets the level of the wine, then leave it for a few minutes. And presto, you've got a less-chilled wine.

2. HOW TO COOL A WINE DOWN QUICKLY

Repeat the exact same process as in previous tip, but use iced water. To test where the temperature is at in either case, take a long plastic drinking straw and dip one end into the wine, then take your finger and place it over the opposite end of the straw. This creates a vacuum and will draw up a small amount of wine into the straw. You can then taste the wine and check its temperature. This is an old bartender trick for testing a cocktail mix but it works just as well if you are looking to check the temperature of a wine.

3. HOW TO FILTER SEDIMENT OUT OF YOUR WINE

Store wines to be decanted upright for a day or two beforehand, so any sediment can settle onto the base. When ready to serve, hold the unopened bottle up to a source of direct light. It could be a candle, lamp, cigarette lighter or a ceiling light. You just need some form of backlighting, which will help you see if the wine is carrying any sediment. Something I always have on hand for decanting is muslin (cheesecloth). Muslin is a soft, loosely knit fabric made from cotton that's long been used in kitchens for fine straining jobs – it's also useful for straining wine, when necessary. You need pieces of it cut into small squares measuring around 10 x 10 cm (4 x 4 inches). Put a clean funnel into your decanter then place layers of the cloth squares inside the funnel, making sure the entire surface is covered evenly. Pour in the wine, making sure you monitor the level of it going in, to avoid spillage. The cloth will filter sediment but will also clog quickly, as the fabric tightens a bit when it becomes wet. Without a funnel you can still strain your wine; you just need to push the cloth into the top of the decanter with your fingers so it forms a pouch or pocket. Then just pour your wine slowly through this.

4. HOW TO TELL WHEN A SCREW-CAP IS 'SCREWED'

Wines sealed under a screw-cap are not impervious to the effects of poor storage. Despite what many wine drinkers think, the part of a screw-cap that protects a wine from spoiling is the small, soft disc that covers the opening of the bottle. The cap, which is the part you screw off, and the 'skirt', which covers the top part of the bottle, are there to protect the cap from being dislodged. If you see any damage to the cap, such as a dent or mark, there is a risk that the disc could have been dislodged and the wine could be affected.

5. DUST AND FINE PARTICLES FLOATING ON THE SURFACE OF YOUR WINE

Not everything can be removed from your wine with muslin (cheesecloth). Dust particles or tiny bits from a cork can all work their way into your wine. If you see any small particles on the surface of your wine in either a glass or decanter, try this technique. Simply get a standard piece of tissue, drape it (flat) across the entire surface of the wine then quickly remove it. You will sacrifice a small amount of wine in this process but the dust and everything else will be gone. If you need to use this technique, do it in a glass after pouring, even if the particles are in a decanter, as the narrow opening of decanters makes it too hard, if not impossible, to do.

6. HOW TO REMOVE A CORK IF YOU DON'T HAVE A CORKSCREW

Screw-top caps are becoming so prevalent that this is less of an issue these days. But it's not unheard of to be confronted with a cork and not have a corkscrew handy. When in a real bind, a few simple handyman tools can help you out. You need a screw, of the type used in building. It should be a long one so it can penetrate most (or all) of the length of the cork, with some length to spare. It doesn't matter what type of head it has on it, that's not important. Using a screwdriver, twist the screw straight into the cork, leaving about 1 cm (½ inch) of the screw poking out of the top of the cork. Slide the protruding bit of the screw between the claws of a hammer and gently pull the cork straight upwards, to work it free. Improvisational – but effective.

Another trick, when you don't have a corkscrew, is pushing the cork back into the bottle. Don't worry about the cork coming into direct contact with the wine – it won't damage the wine or make it taste 'corky'. Take the pointy end of a chopstick and push it down one side of the cork, between the cork and the bottle. Wiggle the chopstick down the side of the cork until it reaches the base of it. This separates the cork from the glass and breaks the vacuum 'seal'. You can then force the cork into the bottle easily with your fingers. Don't use this technique on older bottles with potentially fragile corks, as these can just disintegrate into pieces.

7. OPENING SPARKLING WINE THE SAFEST WAY

Any wine bottled under pressure needs to be approached with care when opening. Spraying a sparkling wine everywhere in a gush of foam may look impressive but frankly, what a waste. I'd rather be drinking it. And there are safety considerations too – if the cork comes out too fast and is pointing in the wrong direction, it can break something or injure someone. Here are some tips.

- A well-chilled sparkling wine that hasn't been agitated or shaken before opening is least likely to fizz or cause the cork to race out uncontrollably.
- Make sure your bottle is on a firm surface when you come to open it. This could be a kitchen bench, a table or even your car bonnet – just as long as it is flat and stable.
- Remove the foil around the top of the bottle.
- Place a hand firmly around the neck of the bottle, using your 'strong' hand for this. So if you are a leftie like me, use your left hand.
- Place the thumb of that hand over the top of the cork. This is for safety; as you work the cork out, you will sense quickly if it is starting to shoot out too fast. Taking your other hand, gently unwind the small piece of wire twisted into a loop around the 'cage' and loosen it. I always leave the wire cage in place over the cork as it acts like a grip around the cork, which can be often wet and slippery from chilling in an ice bucket or from condensation from the refrigerator.
- Tilt the bottle – this is important. There is a small gap between the level of the wine and the bottom of the cork (or screw-cap) in every bottle of wine. In sparkling wines, this air pocket is highly pressurised. If you open the bottle while it is upright, the pressure will escape through the opening at the top of the bottle, often taking some of the wine with it. Taking the hand that's not dealing with the cork end of things, grip the base of the bottle and tilt it at a 45-degree angle or until wine forms a bubble around the air pocket. When this happens, it's safe to open, as the liquid surrounding the air pocket means the pressure can't escape. If you want to get every last drop out of your bottle of bubbles, this is an important step.

- Grip and twist. Grip the cork tightly and twist the bottle firmly but gently from the base, slowly working the cork out. You will feel the pressure building up in the cork behind your thumb. When you feel the cork start to emerge from the bottle, slowly release your thumb pressure. The cork will come out at a speed where you won't get Champagne all over the floor. Or over you.

Keeping it real

I have always brought my work home with me when it comes to entertaining. Service and hospitality put the humanity into a wine experience. Working in restaurants has taught me that this is something we can all do and it makes every bottle of wine, and every meal, taste that little bit better.

This book is intended to be a lifestyle guide, putting wine in a human, rather than a technical context. And that gives you 'permission' to just enjoy wine and make it fit into your life, not become the centre of it, or make it more significant than it ought to be.

WINE IDEAS FOR A PICNIC

SPARKLING

Dry prosecco from Italy

Crémant de Loire from the Loire Valley, France

Crémant de Bourgogne from Burgundy, France

Dry sparkling wine from Tasmania, Australia

WHITE WINES

Vermentino from Sardinia, Italy

Verdejo from Rueda, Spain

Assyrtiko from Santorini, Greece

Picpoul de Pinet from Languedoc, France

Dry riesling from Australia

RED WINES

Pinot noir from Yarra Valley, Australia

Pinot noir from Marlborough, New Zealand

Nebbiolo from Piedmont, Italy

Nebbiolo from Adelaide Hills, Australia

Gamay from Beaujolais, France, or Victoria, Australia

Pinot noir from Burgundy, France

Montepulciano from Campania, Italy

WINE SUGGESTIONS

WINE IDEAS FOR A BARBECUE

WHITE WINES

Picpoul de Pinet from Languedoc, France

Chenin blanc from Vouvray, Loire Valley, France

Garganega from Soave, Italy

Pecorino from Abruzzo, Italy

Albarino from Rías Baixas, Spain

Chardonnay from Long Island, New York State, USA

Chardonnay from Hawkes Bay, New Zealand

Chardonnay from Margaret River, Western Australia

Chardonnay from Saint-Véran, Saint-Aubin
and Mâcon, France

ROSÉ WINES

Crisp and dry to fruity and textural

RED WINES

Barbera from Asti or Alba, Italy

Aglianico from Campania, Italy

Nero d'Avola from Sicily, Italy

Malbec from Mendoza, Argentina

Tempranillo from Rioja, Spain

Gamay from Beaujolais, France

Grenache, shiraz, mourvèdre blends from the southern
Rhône Valley, France

Nebbiolo from Piedmont, Italy

Nebbiolo from Adelaide Hills, South Australia

WINE SUGGESTIONS

WELCOME WINES FOR A DINNER PARTY

SPARKLING WHITE

Non-vintage Champagne from France

Prosecco from Northern Italy

Crémant de Loire from the Loire Valley, France

Crémant de Bourgogne from Burgundy, France

Cava from Catalonia, Spain

SPARKLING WHITE

OR PINK

Pétillant naturel sparkling wine from

USA, France or Australia

FORTIFIED WHITE WINE

Dry sherry (manzanilla) from Jerez, Spain

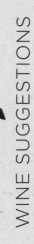

WINE SUGGESTIONS

COLLECTING
WINE

The wines that I collect are those that diarise my own journey in taste. For me they are a far more intimate memory than any 'selfie'.

When sitting in a restaurant, the pressure that many of us feel the moment a wine list is thrust into our hands can be a bit much. At home, there's none of that trepidation. That relaxed sense of confidence that you feel in your own home with wine is so often missing from a wine bar or restaurant experience. Having to quickly make a sensible decision about which wine to choose in formal dining situations can be flustering.

Personally, I love having a wine collection at my fingertips at home. There is something intrinsically personal about all those bottles that I've collected over time. They represent many memories and so much no-pressure enjoyment.

The wines that I collect are those that diarise my own journey in taste. For me they are a far more intimate memory than any 'selfie'. They remind me of places I've been and the people I've spent time with. While this sounds all very romantic, the truth about collecting wine is that it does require you to have a plan. Some foresight and a bit of strategy go a very long way when building a wine collection. As a colleague of mine once said, 'Doing anything right in wine is about preparation, preparation and preparation', and this is nowhere more true than when you are contemplating building a collection.

The word 'cellaring' has given the simple concept of collecting a bad name. As we've discussed earlier in this book, the entrenched language that's used around wine can be intimidating. 'Cellaring' wine implies the need for a dedicated sandstone-encased, lower-level space that's maybe accessible through grand, wrought-iron gates and filled with cobweb-coated bottles of only the finest and rarest vintages. This is simply not true, especially in today's urban areas where high-density housing is redefining traditional lifestyles. Many of us have less space than previous generations did, and the old ideas around a cellar are not really compatible with this.

A working wine collection

I have been buying, building and managing wine collections, for both private clients and restaurants, for over 20 years. These collections ranged in size from a couple of hundred bottles to 18,000 bottles (give or take). Some collections have a monetary value of under a $1000 while some are worth over $5,000,000. What I have learned through study, experience, trial and error is that a considered approach is vital – regardless of the size of, or budget for, the collection. Like a good wine taster, who uses the same approach for a $10 wine as they do for a $100 wine, consistent principles are required to not only build a collection but to keep it growing in terms of both quality and value.

What you want is a 'working' wine collection. This is one that you're constantly dipping in and out of as it serves to incorporate wine into your living habits. It should never be a museum of 'look but don't touch' wines. The collection is designed for you to drink from, not sit and watch bottles age. This holds true for all wine collections, whether personal or professional, small or large. Ask anyone about their favourite wine and they rarely start with a price tag, region or grape variety. They nearly always frame their answer around memories of where they were, what they were eating and who they were with. These lifestyle considerations ought to inform the template you use for populating your wine cellar, even before you begin to engage retailers, go online or visit wineries.

The tips, strategies and objectives used to build professional and commercial cellars are easily translated into a checklist that will help you create a great personal wine collection. Remember, a wine list in a restaurant is merely a shop window for what's in the cellar. The real heart and soul of successful wine culture is in the collating, service and enjoyment of a wine collection. The same philosophy applies to a home collection.

Doing what I do, I get asked a lot by friends and colleagues how to collect wine or build a cellar. The hardest part, I tell them, is deciding where to start. So here is what I would do if you came to me and asked me for help. I would pour a glass of something tasty for us both, get you comfy and ask the following questions.

Where are you storing the wine?

It goes without saying that it all starts with logistics. Even the smallest of floor plans can accommodate a wine collection. With the boom in temperature-controlled refrigeration units, specifically designed for wine drinkers with limited space at home, a tailored storage solution can be found quickly and affordably. But rather than become overly concerned about the place you will store your wine, and let it quickly become more expensive than the wines going into it (as it can), here are some rules that will allow you to utilise existing spaces in your home and start the process without blowing your budget.

TEMPERATURE

Variations in temperature, especially temperature increases, are wine's enemy number one. Wines served too cold need time to warm up in order to release flavours and aromas and taste at their optimum (see page 187). Conversely, if they get too warm they can be forever damaged – and with frightening speed. Never store wine on top of cupboards or anywhere close to a ceiling where warm air will gather (warm air rises). Similarly, don't store wine against walls that are external to the outside of a house, as these attract more heat than internal rooms and walls will. Somewhere near the middle of your floor plan is always best.

Variations in temperature, especially temperature increases, are wine's enemy number one.

LIGHT

Light can damage wines so don't laugh at people who store their favourite wines under their bed. Dark, cool and usually devoid of movement, the space under your bed might not be as crazy a storage solution as you think. Have you ever wondered why wine is generally sold in bottles of coloured, not clear, glass? Tinted glass is a wine's primary defence against light; just like a pair of sunglasses, it's designed to filter out ultraviolet light. When storing wine, you should avoid direct exposure to any form of light but, most importantly, keep it away from fluorescent light. Fluoroescent light can damage a wine within a few days if it is left exposed to it.

MOVEMENT

Moving wines, particularly reds, becomes a more critical factor as wines age. When tannins start to polymerise (become solid), they will 'fall out' and settle in the base of a bottle as sediment. Preventing movement will stop sediment from being disturbed throughout the wine, which can give wine a cloudy appearance – it can also be annoying if bits of it find their way into your glass. It's also possible for white wine to develop a form of sediment, called 'white diamonds'. Essentially, these are crystals of tartaric acid that in high concentration take on a solid form. Sometimes low temperatures can speed up their formation and you'll find these on the underside of a cork – particularly if the bottle has been laid down for an extended period of time. Like sediment in red wine, white diamonds are harmless and not an indicator of wine quality. Actually, you don't see them too often these days as most wine producers put their whites through a process called 'cold stabilisation', where they keep the wines at near-freezing temperatures for 2 weeks. This speeds up the crystal-forming process and any crystals are then filtered out.

What can you afford to spend?

This is a big question and only you know the answer. It all starts with a number – well, two numbers in fact. The first is the amount you can afford in order to start your cellar, and the second is what you can afford each month to keep it going. The initial amount should be seen as purchasing your 'par level', or the number of bottles you feel comfortable with having on hand, on an ongoing basis. The next figure is what you can spend each month to continue to invest in wines, and to replace the bottles you have enjoyed during that month. You don't have to spend the same amount each month, but by allocating a monthly budget, anything you don't spend can go into a 'war chest', which allows your collection to grow either by volume or value, as the opportunity arises.

How much wine do you drink?

Here's another curly question and one that will largely determine the size and range of your collection. Are you someone who likes a glass of wine each day when you come home from work, or do you save up your standard drink allocation for the weekend, and blow it all in one night? Do you like to entertain at home and if so, how often? Do you like to give wine away as gifts? Be realistic when you come up with a number based on your consumption. How much you drink is important, as it helps to manage the size of your collection as well as its cost and content.

Do you like to cook?

I love cooking with wine, and by this I don't mean sloshing a cheap offering into my bolognese sauce for a winey 'kick'. I mean actually drinking a good glass of wine while I am up to my elbows preparing a meal. When I cook I always put on some great tunes; personally, I love Frank Sinatra. I find it gets my culinary juices going and, as I cook, I start to ponder the food, developing ideas around which wines from my collection will work with whatever it is I'm making. As we saw in the Matching food and wine chapter, there can be a real synergy and a common message between what you eat and what you like to drink. If you are a keen cook, your culinary preferences should definitely help inform your wine choices. Here are some considerations around this theme to start you thinking.

- Nearly everyone has a place – or places – whose food they are passionate about and that they love to make at home. Maybe because they've travelled there, and food is a way to serve memory, to reconnect to a certain time and specific place. It could be Italy, France, Thailand, China, South America, North Africa or maybe even Scandinavia. Dominant ingredients and cooking techniques will have a bearing on what wines you'll like to drink with a specific cuisine.
- What about produce? Do you prefer to cook using seafood, poultry, meat, grains or vegetables? Maybe you're vegetarian?
- When you entertain, are you a risk-taker who likes to cook new dishes, or do you prefer to play it safe with things you've cooked hundreds of times before and are completely confident in?
- Everyone has a 'signature dish', something they can whip up in a pinch or when they're craving familiarity after a long week at work. What is yours? And what is the ideal wine to match it with?

By clarifying these things, you'll be closer to determining how much of your wine collection should be geared towards the types of things you like to cook.

Collector categories

Building and stocking a restaurant cellar is guided by a few standard principles, and these can be applied to the home collector in precisely the same way as they are in a restaurant. First, you come up with the broad categories of the wine you want/need and then drill down to specifics. Regardless of the business model of the restaurant, the type of diner it plans to attract, the food and the service style, I would divide wines in a restaurant cellar into three broad categories. Note that each of these categories will be weighted differently in regards to money invested in them, and the amounts of each purchased.

1. TRADERS These are wines that are destined for high turnover, representing styles that are easy drinking and made for quick consumption. At home, these are the equivalent of 'house wines' in a restaurant and they represent those dependable, go-to bottles you reach for when you come home from work, or have to unexpectedly entertain guests. I like to store these separate to my main collection (in the dining room or in my kitchen) so that, when I'm reaching for my staple, go-to drink, I don't feel like I'm always raiding my cellar. Nor will I be tempted to open something more significant from my cellar if the occasion doesn't warrant it. I call this strategy 'impulse control' and it works for me.

2. PREMIUMS These are wines that have a stronger pedigree than traders. They're wines that are regarded as higher quality expressions of a grape variety, a particular vineyard or winemaking. They will have significantly better breeding than your traders and are specific 'food' or 'occasion' wines. They're not really for everyday drinking.

3. INVESTMENTS These are wines purchased with the idea that they will be stored in the cellar and only consumed at later dates when they have aged and increased in quality, and therefore value. The sky's the limit here, but remember to do your research on both the winery and the respective vintage conditions in a region before purchasing. Only a handful of wines are built for the long haul. Depending on contributing factors such as conditions of the specific vintage and the wine quality, these wines can age for years and even decades. Needless to say, these are your 'big' occasion wines, wines to celebrate a milestone or some major life event. The significance of an investment wine, and the specialness around opening it, helps cement the memories of such occasions.

As you can see by now, a clear buying strategy is vital in building a collection. As a sommelier I have had the good fortune to indulge my wildest wine fantasies while someone else has picked up the tab. I have tasted and appreciated wines I would otherwise not have been able to afford. However, I learned very early on that value can, and should, be found at every single price point. An expensive bottle of wine can't necessarily be designated 'better' than a cheaper one – there are excellent wines across the entire spectrum so don't be distracted by price.

For personal wine collections, avoid the trap of accumulating a large cellar – I would much rather have three bottles of cracking wine to drink this week than 3000 bottles I can't touch for 20 years.

I have seen too many restaurants rise and fall on the strength of their wine program, and witnessed the hubris of restaurateurs and sommeliers as they have shopped for their own tastes rather than the needs of their clientele. Don't make the mistake of building a wine collection that looks like an edifice to the opinions of wine experts and wine writers, but one that you can't actually drink for a long time. A collection ought to be about your tastes and your palate and, to a large extent, about your immediate enjoyment. Finding wines that express your sense of personal taste and fit into your lifestyle are the real objectives here.

TRADER WINES

These are not intended for sitting around in your collection for longer than 12 months. These are wines you purchase for their drinkability and up-front fruit character. They should be fresh flavoured, not sweet, and with fruit that's balanced by acidity and soft tannins.

PREMIUMS

These wines should be delicious when they are young, but also possess the structure to age well in the medium term – up to, but not limited to, 6–8 years. These wines should have moderate levels of fruit flavour and acidity (white) or tannin (red). Importantly, these wines should have texture that is shaped and defined by its structural components. I use the word structure when I am talking about the levels of acidity and tannin in a wine. In 'premiums', acidity and tannin are the framework and foundation of the wine. You should be able to taste these in the wine and they should both feel in balance with the other parts of the wine. This is a different quality from the drinkability and immediacy of your trader wines. The wines are more complex by nature, which creates more potential for

When discussing ageing, it is important to note that while all wines will age, they also each have a natural limit for ageing and you can't push a wine beyond that.

food matches. Structure adds not only drinkability but longevity, making them worth the higher price.

INVESTMENTS

By their very nature, these are wines you buy for the long haul – to age. Because they are expensive to make, they represent an investment in time, money and expertise by the producer, and no one does this without factoring in the ability for these types of wines to appreciate in value as time passes. Also, these wines are generally made from grapes grown in the very best vineyards available to the winemaker so, literally from the ground up, the quality is there.

Ageing

When discussing ageing, it is important to note that while all wines will age, they also each have a natural limit for ageing and you can't push a wine beyond that. Those limits vary between regions, varieties and winemakers so it's impossible to be definitive here about how ageing relates to individual styles and types of wine.

The weather conditions around specific vintages are crucial when it comes to the potential a wine has to mature. Yet a winemaker with exceptional skills and insights into their region and vineyards can still produce exceptional wines from average vintages. Equally, a vintage that produces exceptional fruit quality can be butchered by a poor winemaker. You can make bad wine from good fruit but you cannot make good wine from bad fruit.

WHY DO CERTAIN WINES AGE WELL?

As we've previously discussed, everything oxidises. Meat, dirt, wine and even you and I are subject to the degrading effects of prolonged exposure to oxygen. It's a natural and inevitable process, and understanding it better will help you choose wines for your collection.

The best way to describe what wine tastes like as it gets old/oxidises, is to take a green apple and cut it in half. Bite into one half immediately and make a mental note of its flavours and aroma. They're fresh, fruity and – 'appley'. Leave the other half to stand for an hour or so, until the exposed flesh goes brown. Now take a bite. Using the first taste of apple as a benchmark, make mental notes of how the apple's flavour and aroma have changed once it starts to go brown (oxidise). That second apple half, the one that's brown, no longer tastes fresh. Its flavours are muddied and it's not terribly pleasant to eat. This decline in freshness, with something tasting less of itself, is what oxidation tastes like. As we've seen, wines are deliberately exposed to oxygen to varying degrees during their making, and the resulting characteristics actually add to the wine. But they're only a supporting component – if they take over (meaning the wine gets TOO old or oxidised), then that puts the wine in the realms of the faulty.

We live in a time where most wine is bought and consumed within hours of purchase. The idea of maturing wine has not only become something of a novelty but it's also harder to find wines with the characteristics necessary for successful ageing. Wines fuelled by high alcohol, sweet fruit and almost non-existent acid or tannin are great to quaff and eminently drinkable at a young age. However, if you stash these in your cellar, don't expect these 'caterpillars' to transform into 'butterflies' any time soon. By the same token, don't buy a wine with scorching acidity or teeth-shattering tannins and somehow expect time will soften them, turning them into something magical. As I've said before, not all wines improve exponentially with age; some are not meant to be anything more than punchy, easy-drinking wines destined to be consumed young.

A good analogy for how the right wine improves with ageing can be seen in the slow cooking of beef. Take a secondary cut like brisket, which lies over the sternum and ribs of a mature cow. Brisket is a 'load-bearing' cut as it's pivotal in supporting the cow and, as such, is very hardworking. For this reason, it's interlaced with sinewy layers of connective tissue. Therefore, if you were to cook a piece of it like a steak, quickly and over high heat, it would become incredibly tough and chewy. The secret to its tenderness is in long, slow cooking, which enables the connective tissues to break down and melt, making the meat fall-apart tender and complex in flavour in the process.

It's the same for wine. Take cabernet sauvignon, for example. Imagine that the connective tissue in brisket is like the tannin in a cabernet sauvignon, and the slow-cooking process represents time the wine spends in your cellar. With this variety, if you drink it too young, it's like cooking that brisket like a piece of prime eye fillet. It will be 'grippy' (or 'chewy', if it was meat) and extremely hard on the palate. The tannins will still be full of youth and power, while beneath them lie huge concentrations of fruit.

Drink your cabernet sauvignon with the appropriate amount of bottle age, which helps mature and soften the tannins through judicious oxidation, and you then notice the fruit character of the wine. You'll notice too how mouthfeel and flavour will have become softer and a great deal more complex. A unique combination of vintage, variety, region, vineyard and human judgement is required for a wine to age successfully.

THE IMPORTANCE OF BALANCE WHEN AGEING WINE

A good wine will be in balance from day one. For example, if you have a wine that has a lot of oak, that oak can only work if there is enough fruit to support it. If you have a wine singing with high acidity, it too can work but only if there is fruit flavour to support that acid. On the reverse side, a wine can have lots of fruit flavour but if it doesn't have the support of tannin or acidity, it will be simple and sweet and not suitable for long-term drinking.

It's always all about balance. Balance is something more than taste. When a wine is balanced, there is a textural, tactile effect that you detect, long before you begin the subjective exercise of evaluating its flavour and aroma. It's important to reiterate that, while all wines will age the longer they are left in the bottle, not all wines will become better with age. And the potential for any wine ageing always reverts back to that natural balance between acidity, tannins, alcohol and sweetness.

TRADER WHITES

Chardonnay

Riesling

Sauvignon blanc

White blends

Pinot grigio

Vermentino

Semillon

Verdejo

TRADER REDS

Red blends

Gamay

Lagrein

Barbera

Grenache, shiraz, mourvèdre blends

Mourvèdre

Malbec

PREMIUM WHITES

Riesling from Eden Valley, South Australia

White blends from Bordeaux, France

Chardonnay from Margaret River

Riesling from Alsace, France

Chenin blanc from Loire Valley, France

Albarino from Rías Baixas, Spain

Assyrtiko from Greece

Chardonnay from Chablis, France

PREMIUM REDS

Pinot noir from Tasmania

Nebbiolo from Adelaide Hills, South Australia

Grenache from Barossa Valley, South Australia

Cabernet sauvignon and merlot blends from
Margaret River, Western Australia

Grenache, shiraz, mourvèdre blends from the
Barossa Valley, South Australia

Shiraz from Central Victoria, Australia

Barbaresco (nebbiolo) from Piedmont, Italy

Cabernet franc from Loire Valley, France

Tempranillo from Rioja, Spain

Malbec from Mendoza, Argentina

INVESTMENT WHITES

Vintage Champagne

Riesling from Eden Valley and Clare Valley,
South Australia

Riesling from Pfalz, Mosel and the Rheingau,
Germany

Chardonnay from Burgundy, France

INVESTMENT REDS

Pinot noir from Yarra Valley, Victoria, Australia

Pinot noir from Côte de Nuit, Burgundy, France

Nebbiolo from Barolo, Piedmont, Italy

Shiraz and cabernet sauvignon blends from
South Australia

Cabernet sauvignon from Coonawarra 'terra
rossa' belt, South Australia

Red blends from Bordeaux, France

SERVING AGED WINE

Aged wines in restaurants are a dying breed. Like premium wines from Burgundy, Bordeaux and Champagne, only a rare handful of restaurants and wine bars can invest the amounts of cash required to build a well-proportioned collection of aged wine.

Where aged wines really deliver value is in your home, as maturing wine in your home cellar is a satisfying investment. There's nothing like laying down some wines, then anticipating drinking them either in a few months, a year or two, or even decades into the future. And it's not just about ageing the wine and the ultimate taste or smell of it either. For me, putting down some bottles is about the memories I'll create with them, and surely this is wine's greatest power. Collecting and ageing wine requires time and patience and a particular skill in its service too. You don't want to just open aged wines and pour them. Taste the wine. Decant it. As I've previously mentioned, the moment you expose a wine to oxygen it will start to 'open up'. The texture will start to shift, softening the wine and making it more supple. Aroma and flavour will change as the wine evolves and develops in complexity. As this happens, you should keep tasting the wine. This is the fun part – seeing a wine evolve in the glass, right before your very eyes.

HOW LONG DO I WAIT?

A well-curated wine collection will mean you're not salivating at the cellar door, waiting for a bottle to be ready to drink. Your collection should be structured in such a way

MAGNUMS

Collect as much wine as you can in magnums. Why? Because the sheer size of a magnum slows down the ageing process, keeping wines younger and fresher for longer. At 1.5 litres (52 fl oz), they contain twice as much wine as a standard 750 ml (26 fl oz) bottle, but have the same amount of oxygen under the cork – remember, it's that oxygen that ages a wine. Not surprisingly, the ageing process of wine in a magnum takes around one and a half times longer than a 750 ml bottle. I like to encourage people towards magnums, whether they're dining or collecting.

that there's always something ready. And neither variety nor vintage should dictate what you open, but rather the occasion. All the tasting notes, online reviews and social media blasts in the world are no match for putting wine in a glass and sharing the bottle. But, the age-old question remains – you've purchased a case of wine, earmarked it for the cellar and are about to put the bottles to bed. When do you start to drink them?

This is a tricky question to answer as there are so many variables dictating how a wine will transform with bottle age. The best idea, I find, is to purchase at least six to twelve bottles of a particular wine, and open one every year. This way, you are using your sense of taste to bear witness to that wine's evolution, and its journey to maturity. With each wine having its own particular tasting 'window', where the elements of sugar, acid, tannin, alcohol and (perhaps) oak develop and combine to give it a peak of drinkability, the trick is in finding that optimal peak. There is no textbook answer, unfortunately. Some things to look out for are:

IF A WINE IS TOO YOUNG

The wine will be intensely concentrated and textured. It will have potent fruit character but with very little complexity.

IF A WINE IS TOO OLD

The wine will taste dull and might look brownish. There will be a noticeable lack of flavour, weight and concentration.

IF A WINE IS JUST RIGHT

The wine will taste of its components. Sugar, acid, tannin, alcohol and (potentially) oak will all be present, but you will

DRINKING WINDOW

You need to be aware of the 'drinking window' when you open a bottle of aged wine. Wine continues to open up until it hits optimum drinking point, and the only way to chart exactly when this happens is to keep tasting it. Wines that are youthful and fruity will have a larger tasting window, because the effects of oxygen on them take place slowly. The older the wine, the smaller the window, as tannins have already exerted their softening influence and there will be less resistance to oxygen. If you have more than one bottle of a particular wine, keep a note of how it changes in the glass once you've poured it, so next time you will know how long it needs to open up for optimal drinking. The best way to know the current state of a wine, in terms of drinkability and maturity, is always to open a bottle.

find it hard to pick out any dominant element. Depending on the wine, such maturity can occur at the 2-year mark ... or it could take 20 years. It all depends on the individual wine.

THE 'PLATEAU'

As we've just seen, all wines have this window of optimum drinkability, where the effect of maturation yields its most positive results. Many wines made today have a rather short window, such as sauvignon blanc from Marlborough in New Zealand. Other wines, like the red cabernet blends from Bordeaux in France, with their high concentration of tannin, can age for decades. But their window of peak drinkability is actually at around the 15 to 20 year mark. When shopping for aged wines, be sure to ask about the drinking windows for the ones you intend to collect.

Creating your wine collection brief

OK, now we have worked through the practical logistics: how much you drink, what you want to spend, where food fits into the equation and how much you like to entertain –now it's time to put all this information into a brief.

This document will become your set of Wine Commandments, a checklist that ensures you remain on track, style-wise and budget-wise. It will become your guideline when you are ready to go shopping. Trust me; going into a good bottle shop without a budget and a plan is like ordering from a great menu when you're ravenous. Eyes can be way bigger than stomachs and you can easily find yourself ordering well beyond your capacity and your budget. This 'brief' can be either succinct, or detailed and drawn out. Putting all we have discussed in this chapter into a document will let you take the first step in building a great personal wine collection.

SAMPLE BRIEF

Below is an example of a brief I wrote for a private client, who came to me looking to grow their personal wine collection. This will, I hope, give you insight into the kinds of things to think about for your own brief.

The clients are a professional working couple who live in an apartment and who enjoy cooking both Mediterranean and Asian-inspired foods. They entertain at home weekly. Both like to eating out regularly and see restaurants and wine bars as an important part of their social life. They have approximately $1000 ready to invest in setting up their cellar, with approximately $500 per month to spend on its growth and upkeep. They are very keen to learn about wine and have developed a strong interest in wine with an 'x factor', but also like to revert to established wines and wine regions for certain occasions.

DRINK They currently buy in small but regular amounts, but would like to drink more wine and drink better wine. They nearly always drink wine with food, rarely drinking it on its own.

EAT She's proficient in the kitchen and enjoys cooking, working with potent flavours and spices at times. He is Indian – spicy dishes and curries are favourites. Both enjoy seafood and chicken as core proteins, with cheese an almost compulsory finish to a dinner party rather than dessert.

DRINKING AT HOME They entertain regularly and have a good, dedicated space set aside for formal dining.

DRINKING WHEN OUT They regularly eat at good restaurants both socially and for work. They also regularly dine at friends' homes and take wine as a gift.

LOGISTICS Good storage is available in the cupboard in the central part of the floor plan, with low heat and light due to the space being away from any exterior walls. A custom racking system would suit.

BUYING STRATEGY More variation, with wines suited to a variety of occasions. Purchase wine in two stages, with 50 per cent of total bottles purchased at each stage.

CURRENTLY Have zero bottles. There is potential space for 120 bottles.

Based on all the information above, I came up with the following suggested breakdown of their collection:

- 60 per cent (72 bottles) trader wines
- 30 per cent (36 bottles) premiums
- 10 per cent (12 bottles) investments

Remember that this first purchase is the 'par level', which is the number of wines you purchase to start a cellar. If in the following month you only drink six bottles, then you can replace them and your costs for the month are low. Also, if your lifestyle changes, you can change the mix between traders, premiums and investments, or even the size of the cellar if you wish to collect more or are drinking less. I want to be clear – when I say 'working cellar' I mean one you engage with and drink from regularly. It's a project not to make money from or to build a museum.

1. TRADER WINES

With a lifestyle built around spontaneity and a passion for food, this couple needs wines that are adaptable to regular drinking across varied occasions but not in big amounts. I would suggest:

SPARKLING
Prosecco from Italy

WHITE
Light- to medium-bodied wines with high natural acidity and little or no oak. Avoid too much fruit or alcohol – the focus is on freshness.
Riesling from South Australia
Vermentino from Sardinia, Italy
Verdejo from Spain

RED
Light-bodied examples with high acidity, juicy fruit flavours and a 'cleansing' feeling on the palate.
Gamay from Beaujolais, France
Pinot noir from Mornington Peninsula, Victoria
Nerello mascalese from Mount Etna, Sicily

2. PREMIUMS

These wines should be delicious when young, but also possess the structure to age well. Wines would need to be more diverse than traders or investments, as they will need to fit with the lifestyle of the clients, especially where eating, cooking and entertaining are concerned. Some wines should suit the delicate nature of seafood and others should support heavier proteins such as beef and lamb. These wines should have moderate levels of fruit flavour and acidity (white) or tannin (red). With the influence of the Mediterranean (salt and oil) and Indian (spice, warmth and richness) flavours in their cooking, I suggest a diverse collection of wines that offer varying levels of fruit concentration, acidity and tannin, along with that all-important drying or 'savoury' quality for optimum food compatibility. For this reason and the clients' desire for a bit of an 'x factor', I look to include white wines with slightly oxidised characters.

WHITE

White blends from the Rhône Valley and southern France

Chardonnay from Chablis, France

Chardonnay (oxidised) from Jura, France

Chenin blanc from the Loire Valley, France

Albarino from Rías Baixas, Spain

RED

Pinot noir from Tasmania, Australia

Nebbiolo from Langhe, Italy

Grenache, shiraz, mourvèdre blends from the Rhône Valley, France

Barbaresco (nebbiolo) from Piedmont, Italy

Cabernet franc from the Loire Valley, France

Tempranillo from Rioja, Spain

Malbec from Mendoza, Argentina

3. INVESTMENTS

I'm looking for the best examples from particular vineyards, where the winemaker showcases the vineyard in the glass.

Wines are generally made from grapes grown in the very best vineyards and will have a better sense of balance between acidity, tannin, fruit concentration, texture and body. I'll choose wines with good balance for drinking now, but ones where the peak will only show with some age.

WHITES
Single vineyard Hunter Valley semillon, Australia
Single vineyard riesling (with some sweetness)
from Mosel, Germany
Single vineyard chardonnay from Burgundy, France
REDS
Pinot noir from Burgundy, France and Oregon, USA
Syrah from New Zealand
Cabernet sauvignon from Coonawarra 'terra rossa'
belt, Australia
Barbaresco (nebbiolo) from Piedmont, Italy

TEAM WINE

A great way to begin the process of building your wine collection is to engage the support of your local wine shop. Make them your 'wine buddy'. They could work at a boutique wine store but remember that even big liquor chains have some really knowledgeable wine service professionals patrolling the shop floor. Give them your brief and see what they come back with. And if their suggestions are on the money, they can become an invaluable asset over time as they get to know your taste and budget.

A new wine language

Buying, collecting and, in many cases, ageing wine is not only affordable but an amazing part of the dining, drinking and entertaining experience. Working with wine in your own home gives you the freedom to learn and experiment. It also allows you to drink wines that are about you, your taste and your journey in food and wine.

The new rules in wine are, in my opinion, built on a new language that's written into the total wine experience, not just into wine itself. Cooking, eating, music, service, collecting, entertaining, discussing and sharing – these are all pivotal to the wine experience –and the language around wine needs to reflect this. This is the new charter for wine drinkers, where there are no real beginners or experts and where enjoying wine is, above all, a social undertaking.

ACKNOWLEDGMENTS

This book, like my life, is a product of desperation, desire and a good dose of blind luck. There are a lot of people to thank without whom the idea for this book would still be sitting on the back of a beer coaster. Thank you Terry Durack and Jill Dupleix, who saw the potential, and Murdoch Books who brought it to life. Thanks to my mentors, Charles Leong, Craig Hemmings and Guillaume Brahimi, for the lessons and values. Thank you to 'Kev' – wherever you are – and to the restaurants who gave me a home when I needed one. Most of all, thank you to my wife, Jeanine, for your love, support, guidance, patience and the kick in the arse.

Published in 2017 by Murdoch Books, an imprint of Allen & Unwin

Murdoch Books Australia
83 Alexander Street,
Crows Nest NSW 2065
Phone: +61 (0)2 8425 0100
murdochbooks.com.au
info@murdochbooks.com.au

Murdoch Books UK
Ormond House,
26–27 Boswell Street,
London WC1N 3JZ
Phone: +44 (0) 20 8785 5995
murdochbooks.co.uk
info@murdochbooks.co.uk

For corporate orders and custom publishing contact our business
development team at salesenquiries@murdochbooks.com.au

Publisher: Diana Hill
Manuscript Development: Leanne Kitchen
Editorial Manager: Emma Hutchinson
Editor: Ariana Klepac
Design Manager: Madeleine Kane
Design & illustrations: Alissa Dinallo
Production Manager: Lou Playfair

ISBN 978 1 74336 838 1 Australia
ISBN 978 1 74336 839 8 UK
A cataloguing-in-publication entry is available from the catalogue
of the National Library of Australia at nla.gov.au
A catalogue record for this book is available from the British Library

Colour reproduction by Splitting Image Colour Studio Pty Ltd,
Clayton, Victoria
Printed by 1010 Printing International, China